HARDPRESS.NET

ISBN: 9781290714549

Published by:
HardPress Publishing
8345 NW 66TH ST #2561
MIAMI FL 33166-2626

Email: info@hardpress.net
Web: http://www.hardpress.net

A HISTORY OF SICILY

491–289 B.C.

The Tutorial Series.—B.A., 1891.

(*Ready early in* 1890.)

B.A. Latin Notabilia and Test Papers for 1891, on the Prescribed AUTHORS and SPECIAL PERIOD of History. **1s. 6d.**

B.A. Greek Notabilia and Test Papers for 1891, on the Prescribed AUTHORS and SPECIAL PERIOD, including a List of the more difficult Greek Verbal Forms. **1s. 6d.**

Cicero—De Finibus, Book I. Edited with Explanatory NOTES and an INTRODUCTION. By S. MOSES, M.A. Oxon. and B.A. Lond., Assistant Examiner in Classics at the University of London. **3s. 6d.**

Cicero—De Finibus, Book I. A TRANSLATION. **2s.**

Cicero—De Finibus, Book I. TEXT, NOTES, and TRANSLATION (*complete*). **5s.**

Terence—Adelphi. A TRANSLATION. **2s.**

History of the Reigns of Augustus and Tiberius, with an Account of the Literature of the Period. By A. H. ALLCROFT, B.A. Oxon., and W. F. MASOM, B.A. Lond. **2s. 6d.**

Synopsis of Roman History, B.C. 31—A.D. 37, with short Biographies of Eminent Men. By W. F. MASOM, B.A. Lond., and A. H. ALLCROFT, B.A. Oxon. **1s.**

Euripides—Iphigenia in Tauris. A TRANSLATION. By G. F. H. SYKES, B.A. Lond., Assistant-Examiner in Classics at the University of London. **2s. 6d.**

Plato.—Phaedo. A TRANSLATION. **3s. 6d.**

History of Sicily, B.C. 490—289, from the Tyranny of Gelon to the Death of Agathocles, with a History of Literature. By A. H. ALLCROFT, B.A. Oxon., and W. F. MASOM, B.A. Lond. **3s. 6d.**

Synopsis of Sicilian History, B.C. 491—289. By A. H. ALLCROFT, B.A. Oxon., and W. F. MASOM, B.A. Lond. **1s.**

B.A. English Examination Questions on all the Pass Subjects set for 1891. **2s.**

Univ. Corr. Coll. Tutorial Series.

A HISTORY
OF SICILY

491—289 B.C.

BY

A. H. ALLCROFT, B.A. Oxon.,

FIRST CLASS HONOURMAN IN CLASSICS,

EDITOR OF HORACE' ODES, LIVY XXI., SOPHOCLES' ANTIGONE, ETC. ;

AND

W. F. MASOM, B.A. Lond.,

FIRST CLASS HONOURMAN IN CLASSICS, UNIVERSITY EXHIBITIONER,

EDITOR OF HERODOTUS VI., ODYSSEY XVII., TACITUS' ANNALS I.

LONDON : W. B. CLIVE & CO.,

UNIV. CORR. COLLEGE PRESS WAREHOUSE,

13 BOOKSELLERS ROW, STRAND, W.C.

CONTENTS.

A HISTORY OF SICILY.

---◇---

.CHAPTER I.

The Carthaginians.

Origin of the Phœnicians—Phœnicia—Mercantile Character of the
People — Their Trade — Colonies — Carthage — Its Position and
Growth—The Carthaginian Empire—Topography of Carthage—Its
Fortifications—Change in the Policy of Carthage—Early Relations
with Sicily—Armies—Government and Constitution—Weaknesses
of Carthage—Mercenary Troops—Cruelty to Unsuccessful Generals
—Religion—Influence on Greece of the Phœnicians in Religion—In
Art—Carthaginian Literature—Remains.

THE history of the island of Sicily has been that of a
struggle between European and Asiatic races for the
possession of the most fertile island in the Mediterranean
basin. In earlier days Greeks and Carthaginians, in
later days Normans and Saracens, were the combatants;
and the peace of the island has been secure only when
it has been recognised as the dependency of some mighty
Continental power, whether in Africa or in Europe.

The earliest race to interfere with the primitive inhabitants of Sicily were the Phœnicians.* Akin to the
Hebrews, and a member of the family of nations called
Semitic, the Phœnicians dwelt originally about the upper
shores of the Persian Gulf, where the islands of Bahrein
and Arad still contain the tombs of a multitudinous

---

* The name Phœnicia is derived from the Greek Φοῖνιξ, either in the significa-
tion of a 'palm-tree,' from the abundance of those trees about Tyre, etc., or in
that of 'red,' from the complexion of the people. The Latin form is *Pœnus*,
and its derived adjective *Punicus*, both meaning, not Phœnician, but Carthaginian.

people, and were, perhaps, the sacred necropolis of the race. As early, however, as 2800 B.C., they left these lands and wandered westward until they found a home on the shore of the Mediterranean, in the narrow slip of coast which was known to the Jews as the land of the Philistines and Tyrians, to the Greeks as Phœnicia, to later peoples as Syria or Palestine. The cause of their emigration is said to have been the prevalence of earthquakes, but the growth of the power of Chaldæa may have been at least one factor in the result. They brought away with them the memory of their older homes, and in their new land they founded an Aradus and a Tyrus to perpetuate the names of two of the islands of the Red Ocean,* whence they came.

The territory of Phœnicia is a mere belt of coast land, never exceeding twenty miles in width, and averaging only one mile. In length it measured in its greatest extent 180 miles, taking Gabala (*Jebel*) as the northern, and Carmel as the southern limit; but it is more usual to regard as the limits Aradus on the north, Tyre on the south. The land, if narrow, was exceedingly fertile and well watered, and was, moreover, defended from attack on the land side by the natural double barrier of Libanus (*Lebanon*) and Anti-Libanus. Spurs of the Lebanon range run down to the coast at frequent intervals, and divide the land with additional barriers; and the jutting headlands scarcely leave room for the construction of a continuous road along the coast. But these barriers were valued only as keeping off the incursions of the nomads beyond, and the Phœnicians never utilized them, as they might have done, as the bulwarks of a national liberty. They were a nation of traders. They had no care for empire, and, indeed, they were never sufficiently numerous to have made head against the mightier nations of Babylon, Nineveh, Persia, and Egypt. They desired only so much space as should provide them with a home, whence they might sail to explore the farthest shores. From the very earliest times they must have been a com-

---

* The name Mare Erythræum, or Rubrum, was given, not to the Red Sea, but to the Persian Gulf.

mercial people, for their island-homes in the Persian Gulf still remain the natural emporium of the trade between Europe and the Indian coasts. They may have maintained this trade by means of caravans, for we know they had a constant intercourse with the Assyrian monarchy; they certainly opened new routes towards the west, and rapidly monopolized the entire commercial wealth of the Mediterranean. They made no conquests by war, but quietly extended their factories and trading-stations from island to island through the Ægean to the coasts of Greece, along the shores of Macedonia, by Thasos and Samo-Thrace, even to the Black Sea. Most of all they were attracted by the precious metals and the *murex*, a shellfish which furnished them with the famous dye known as 'Tyrian purple.' In quest of one or other of these objects they came to Cyprus and Chalcis of Euboea, rich in copper ores; to Thasos, where their gold-diggers 'overturned a whole mountain'; to Laurium, where they brought to light and gathered the best treasures of the silver-mines afterwards so valuable to Athens; to Trœzen and Hermione for *murex*. The names of Megara and Samos, of Macaria, the fountain of Marathon, of the Cadmea, the Acropolis of Thebes, all bear witness to their presence; while scarce an important name in Crete or Cyprus but is Phœnician. From the eastern and southern shores of Hellas they passed along the western coast, leaving their records even at Olympia, the stronghold of Hellenism, in Corcyra, and in the regions of Epirus about the ancient oracle of Dodona; and so, still westward, to Italy and Sicily. The year 1500 B.C. saw them established at many points upon the western shore of Italy, notably at Punicum, in Etruria. Thence they advanced to Sardinia and Corsica, to Spain, and to Africa, where, in 1140 B.C., they founded their first factory of Utica, on the Gulf of Tunis.

This westward bent was due not only to innate enterprise and quest of traffic, but also to the fact that the Hellenes of the eastern Mediterranean were now waking up to emulation, and gradually ousting the Phœnicians from the islands and mainland of Greece. The Phœnicians retired, seemingly without a struggle. They had gathered the best that was to be got, and could cheerfully leave the pickings to others. All the west lay open to them, and thither they turned with fresh energies. Sicily was fringed with their stations, and all the islands north and west of Sicily were ransacked by their merchants. Finally Spain presented to them a virgin land teeming with precious metals, and there, before the year 1000 B.C., they founded the town of Gades (*Cadiz*), the centre of that land of Tarshish whence they brought gold for the temple of Solomon in Jerusalem.

So wide and continuous a commercial activity drew to Phœnicia the wealth of the world. Her merchants were ' the princes of the earth.' Through their hands passed all that was marketable from India and Assyria, Arabia and Egypt, and all the nations of Europe and Africa. The two original colonies of Tyre and Sidon grew to a wealth that was proverbial, and other towns, such as Aradus, Berytus, Byblus, and smaller places, shared in the national prosperity. Even the conquests of Asshur-izir-pal and Sennacherib did not affect the prosperity of a people who submitted readily to the rule of any power so that they might pursue in peace their mercantile calling. They lived apart in their towns, each under its own petty king, with laws of its own. Tyre had indeed a nominal ascendancy, but there was no actual unity. Yet to such a power did even the single cities attain, that Tyre's king, Ethbael, could give his daughter as a wife to Ahab, King of Samaria. Ahab fell fighting with the Syrians against Assyria, about 850 B.C., and Phœnicia was annexed by Shalmanezer II. ; but three years previously there had been some intestine troubles in Tyre, and a body of expelled citizens had fled to Africa, where they founded, 853 B.C., Kirjath-Hadeschath, ' the New Town,' ten miles from Utica, the older city. Kirjath-Hadeschath became in Greek Carchedon, and in Latin Carthago—the Carthage of history.

According to the story in Virgil, Sychæus, King of Tyre, was murdered by his brother-in-law Pygmalion, and his widow, Elissa or Dido fled secretly, with a band of wealthy Tyrians whom the cruelty and rapacity of the usurper forced to seek safety elsewhere. All we can certainly say is that Carthage was a direct offshoot from Tyre, and that it never forgot its filial duty towards the mother city. Thither was sent a yearly tithe to the temple of Tyrian Hercules, and when Tyre was taken by Alexander the Great, in 332 B.C., the refugees found a welcome within the walls of Carthage.

The new colony was situated on the southern shore of the Bay of Tunis, about thirty miles distant from the modern town of Tunis, and a few miles southward of the estuary of the Bagradas (*Mejerda*). In the heart of the most fertile region of the African coast, it was admirably fitted to be the home of the merchant princes who spent in quiet country enjoyments the gains of earlier commercial efforts ; while its bay furnishes almost the only safe harbour on the whole coast from Alexandria to the Pillars of Hercules (*Gibraltar*). Eastward the promontory of Heræum (*Cape Bon*) juts out towards Sicily, from which it is but ninety miles away, and beyond lay the great indentation known to the ancients as the Greater and Lesser Syrtes, or 'Drifts,' from the shoals and sand-banks which stretched along the coast. The coast itself was then, as now, little better than a sandy desert for a distance of 800 miles. After this, the fertile lands of Cyrenaica were reached, conterminous with the western boundaries of Egypt. In contrast with the desolation of the eastern desert was the wonderful productiveness of the coast westward from Cape Bon. Here it was no uncommon thing for crops to yield one hundred-and-fifty-fold, and even now the provinces of Tunis, Algeria, and Morocco retain something of their ancient luxuriance. But there is no reason to suppose that the founders of Carthage chose the site of the new town only for its fertility. It possessed inestimable advantages as a centre for trade, commanding as it did the whole of the eastern and western basins of the Mediterranean, and the resources of continental Africa to boot. The soil was left in the hands of the native Libyans, to whom the Carthaginians even paid a yearly tribute—the rental of their holding; and it was to commerce that the new city was devoted. And the growth of that commerce was marvellous. Three hundred factories stretched round the western shoulder of Africa, and the traders of Carthage penetrated beyond the Canaries to the Cameroons, whence they brought back captive gorillas, ivory and gold, and stories of the fiery Cameroons mountain.* Spain, with its mines of silver, iron, and quicksilver, was almost a home to them. They reached even to the Scilly Isles, where they purchased the tin of Cornwall, and to the Baltic, whence they brought home amber. The products so obtained they wrought into vessels and implements whose design was borrowed from the inventiveness of Greece, of Egypt, and of the East, but whose beauty of workmanship was entirely Phœnician. They were inimitable imitators; insomuch that to the Greeks of Homer's day all that was artistic was Phœnician, for it came to them through the hands and from the forges of the Tyrians and their descendants.

Within a hundred years of the reputed foundation of Carthage, Sicily and Sardinia were regarded as her provinces, together with Malta, and the Lipari and Balearic Isles. With increase of wealth came increase of territory. The tribute was no longer paid to the Libyans, but they were in their turn reduced to the position of serfs who tilled the soil of the immediate vicinity—the home province—for their masters, and occupied the territories beyond as tributary dependencies. The intermarriage of Carthaginians with native Libyans gave rise to a half-breed population called Libyo-Phœnicians, who occupied the 300 cities of the home-province, but were treated with the same harshness as the pure Africans, and not allowed to fortify their towns. Utica was the one exception to this jealous rule, and there the native Phœnician element was doubtless too prominent to allow any fear of disaffection. From Aræ-Philæni, on the coast of the Great Syrtis, to the Atlantic, the whole region was tributary to Carthage, and so heavy was the tribute, that as much as fifty per cent. of the year's pro-

* Periplus of Hanno.

duce was exacted in a time of need, and the town of Leptis, itself a direct colony from Tyre, paid a talent *per diem*.

The city of Carthage itself clustered round the citadel, Bosra (Canaanitish, *a fort*), which stood upon rising ground at the extremity of a sort of peninsula formed by two lagoons opening into the Gulf of Tunis. A massive outer wall crossed this peninsula from north to south, while the citadel and the Cothon, or naval harbour at its foot, were surrounded on the landward side by a second wall of immense strength. Forty-five feet in height on the outer side, and furnished at intervals of 200 feet with lofty towers, the wall was backed by a second and a third line of solid masonry; and the space between, partitioned and divided into two stories, could stable 300 elephants with their stores of forage in the basement, and over these 4,000 horses. Barracks for 20,000 infantry completed this wall, which joined the ring-wall of the Bosra itself. The Cothon was an artificial basin containing docks for 220 ships of war, having in the centre the admiral's island residence. It opened into the mercantile harbour, of still larger dimensions; and this again into the bay.

Such fortifications and harbourage so large imply an immense population. What it may have been at the time when the strength of Carthage was unimpaired we cannot say; but at the date of the Third Punic War (146 B.C.), when the intermittent warfare of three and a half centuries had doubtless thinned the ranks of the native Carthaginians, there still remained 700,000 souls within the walls. It was unusual, indeed, for the citizens to serve in war, although special privileges were offered to induce them to do so. Nevertheless, several occasions will occur in this history when a large citizen force was levied; and on one such occasion at least (B.C. 394-5) it suffered virtual annihilation. In the year 310 B.C. a force of 40,000 native foot and 3,000 horse and chariots marched out to meet the advance of Agathocles.

The Carthaginians, however, were not men of war, but of traffic, like their parents the Phœnicians, and, as has been said, that nation preferred to retire without resistance when they were no longer left in peaceful possession of their trading-stations. But when, after ceding thus tacitly the whole of the Eastern Mediterranean trade to the Greeks, they found that that people were menacing the Phœnician preserves in the west, they were constrained to alter their policy. As will be seen, they did so too late. The first Greek settlers landed in Sicily in 735 B.C., but it was not until a century and a half later that an effort was made by the Carthaginians to oust them from what had now become virtually a Greek island. The statesman to whom was due the new policy was named Mago; and it was under his guidance that Carthage turned her attention first to the establishment of her supremacy in Africa, *circa* 530 B.C. This done, she entered on aggressive wars in Sardinia and in Sicily. The former island was reduced by Hasdrubal, son of Mago; the Hamilcar who fell at Himera 480 B.C. was a second son. But by this time the rapid development of the Hellenes in Sicily had restricted the Carthaginians to the western corner of the island, where were situated their three great marts of Motye, Solus, and Panormus. Until the close of the First Punic War, 241 B.C., they retained always so much of the island, and at times extended their influence for brief seasons over a much larger area. But to the Greeks they were a hated nation, with whom could be no compromise; and in suffering Hellenic influence to spread unchecked for 150 years, they forfeited their power in Sicily. With the Sicels, on the other hand, they could and did live on good terms, for they cared only to command the coast, while the Sicels had no tendency to maritime pursuits.

More fatal to their success than any error of judgment was their system of warfare. The disinclination of the citizens to serve was met by hiring mercenaries who had no interest in the results of the war beyond their stipulated hire, and who might at any moment transfer their services to a higher bidder. Collected from the nomad Libyans, the Libyo-Phœnicians, from Spain, Gaul, Etruria, Liguria, and Italy, even from the Hellenes themselves, they formed armies of undoubted fearlessness and of redoubtable numbers. Armies of from 150,000 to 300,000 men were not unusual with the Carthaginians. But they lacked all the moral strength of war—unity of blood and language, attachment to their leader; above all, attachment to the country which they professed to serve. Their very numbers rendered them unmanageable to the run of Carthaginian commanders, who had no talent for war or diplomacy. Levied in the spring, they were disbanded in the autumn; and thus was lost the only means of creating a fictitious patriotism amongst them—permanency of service. Mercenary troops were the weapon of the Sicilian despots also, but they were a weapon never laid aside—retained and cherished until they learnt to identify their own interests with that of their masters.

The Balearic Isles and Spain provided the best slingers the world ever saw; the Ligurians were the ideal of light troops; while the more stalwart Sabellians and Etruscans of Italy furnished an infantry akin to that with which Rome conquered the world. The African tribes supplied a superb light cavalry that was inexhaustible. The Libyo-Phœnicians rode into battle in chariots of iron, and behind them followed the elephants, which routed even the Romans in more than one battle. Such a force, supported as it usually was by a flotilla whose very war-vessels were counted by thousands, and whose transports were limitless, was after all of little value. It was little superior to the motley horde of millions that served under the Persian banners—superior only in so far as Western blood is sterner than that of the East.

The government of Carthage was a close oligarchy, whose members were the descendants of the original colonists from Tyre, forming a class similar to the patricians of early Rome.* Of these, twenty-eight chosen members formed the council, and two others, elected for life, were the actual heads of the State. The title of the latter was *Shophet* (plural, *Shophetim*), which became in

* There are said to have been 3 tribes, 30 *curiæ*, and 300 *gentes* at Carthage, exactly corresponding to those of Rome; but such a *theoretical* class-system is not an unusual feature of early States.

Latin *Suffes* (plural, *Suffĕtes*) ; and they were compared by Aristotle to the two kings of Sparta, and by Latin writers to the Roman consuls. The latter parallel is probably the truer, for the two suffetes were doubtless a contrivance for limiting the excessive power of a sole monarch—the form of government in the mother city, Tyre, and therefore presumably the original form at Carthage also. The council declared war, made peace, appointed the commanders in war, and in general administered the affairs of the entire State, while the suffetes acted as their executive, occasionally even leading the army in person.* The mass of the populace, the Demos, were without privileges, and virtually without voice in the government ; though in theory, if the suffetes and the council disagreed, the question was decided by an appeal to the masses.

Such appears to have been the constitution of Carthage in the earliest form of which we have any knowledge. But in the nature of things such a constitution could not remain unaltered, particularly in a mercantile State. Mercantile pursuits engender a spirit of liberalism or democracy amongst their votaries in proportion as the latter are naturally more or less inclined to political activity. Such activity was never a characteristic of the Phœnicians, and hence the mass of them did not, like the ' sea-going mob ' of Athens, push their claims to self-government. But the oligarchy contained in itself the causes of change. A council (*gerusia*) of twenty-eight members, chosen for life, afforded too little play for any political bent in the ranks of a rich, powerful, and numerous aristocracy ; while such as it did possess was limited by the virtual absolutism of the suffetes. The offices of gerusiast and suffete, and consequently those of general and admiral, fell alike into the hands of one or two families of special distinction, to the exclusion of their fellow-nobles ; and the latter used their best efforts to secure a more substantial voice in the government. It was the ascendency of Mago and his sons, above alluded to, which gave them the actual pretext for the erection

* *E.g.*, Hamilcar at Himera, 480 B.C.

of a second council of 104 members, termed judges, who controlled the original council, just as the latter controlled the suffetes. Like the aristocratic council of the Areopagus at Athens, the original council of Carthage was gradually superseded, and their power transferred to The Hundred, as they were loosely called. This body exercised now an absolutism so complete that they are compared to the Ephors of Sparta, before whose authority the gerusia (council) and the two kings were alike in later times helpless. With The Hundred rested the audit of the actions of gerusiasts, suffetes, and generals alike; and they seem to have purposely avoided office themselves, content to enjoy the control of others. Thus at the time when the struggle of Carthage with the Greeks commences, the constitution of the city was still an oligarchy of the closest kind, though the actual centre of power had shifted to a somewhat larger, if no less irresponsible, body than the original council.

Thus much is, in brief, all that is known of a government of which Aristotle says that its stability was something to admire, inasmuch as he could find no occasion on which it had been seriously endangered even by one of its own members aiming at the despotism. Indeed, it seems to have been mild and equitable at least towards the Carthaginians themselves. One instance will occur, but at a later date than that at which Aristotle wrote, of an attempt to establish a monarchy;* but it met with no support from the populace, the very class which would seem at first sight most likely to resent their own inferiority and seek to be revenged on the ruling oligarchy. The worst enemies of Carthage were her despised African subjects, upon whom fell the burden of a heavy taxation, for which they received nothing in return. The Libyans never forgot that the Carthaginian was an invader and an aggressor; and more than once their rising brought the mighty city to the brink of ruin. The Phœnicians of Africa had no genius for amalgamation and pacification, any more than had their fellows of Phœnicia proper, and it was to this incapacity they owed the perils brought

* That of Bomilcar, 309 B.C.

2

upon them by Agathocles, and that final ruin from which Scipio earned the title of Africanus.

Yet other causes of weakness were inherent in the military system already described. The mercenary troops, so difficult to handle and only to be kept in allegiance by success and the plunder which it brought, were always liable to turn on the masters who had bought their services. No patriotism stood in their way. To them Carthage was as legitimate a field of plunder as were the enemies whom they were hired to chastise. And equally dangerous was the blind and cruel policy of The Hundred, who avenged upon an unsuccessful general the results of ill-fortune or incompetency, yet who were never at pains to appoint to the command a man of military ability. The cases of the three great Barcines, Hamilcar, Hasdrubal, and Hannibal, are exceptional, and belong to a later age. At the date with which we are now dealing the general was appointed apparently without any thought for his fitness. If he was successful, so much the better for Carthage and for him ; but if he failed, he paid for his failure with his life, nailed to a cross as an example, and the sins of the father were even visited upon the children with the same inhumanity. One of themselves, though he suffered in this manner for flagrant treason, could yet warn his countrymen as they saw him hanging on the cross that such a policy could never bring success.* It deterred what few able generals the nation possessed from serving so unjust a mistress, and caused the leader to think less of his country's honour than of his own security.

Like most of the old Oriental nations, the Phœnicians tended towards a gloomy and morbid cruelty, and the vindictiveness of their treatment of a Gisco or a Bomilcar was but the reflection of their religious ceremonials—the ' abomination of the Sidonians.' Their great deity was Baal, or Bel, the Moloch of the Bible, God of the Sun. His consort was Astarte, or Tanith, Goddess of the Moon, sometimes surnamed Mulitta. The former was the God to whom they sacrificed human victims, usually

* Bomilcar.

infants, who were laid in the outstretched hands of an image so constructed that, when a fire was kindled within, their bodies fell backwards into the flames. The state sacrifices in honour of Baal were the chosen children of the noblest families, and when, on the occasion of Agathocles' invasion, it was discovered that the promptings of affection had induced some parents to keep back their own children and offer in their stead the purchased children of base-born and less humane parents, the pious fraud was condoned by a holocaust of two hundred infants. It was this practice, long ago extinct amongst the Hellenes, which roused so fiercely their detestation for the Phœnicians at large; and it was from this God that so many Carthaginian names derive their termination—*bal*.*

Hardly less debasing was the worship of Astarte, the Phœnician Venus, and not improbably the original source of the Greek Aphrodite and Roman Venus. Closely connected with the cult of Adonai (Adonis), it early found its way into Greece, where Corinth attained an unenviable notoriety for a ritual entirely un-Greek in its impurity. Corinth, indeed, was particularly the centre of Phœnician tradition in Central Greece, for here was worshipped Melicertes, identical even in name with the Phœnician Melcarth.† He was worshipped with no bloody sacrifices, or at least with none of human blood, and his temples contained no image. Tyre was especially his city, and there Herodotus saw its pillars of emerald and gold; but Thasos, too, had a famous temple in his honour, and at Gades, in the far west, Hannibal registered to him vows for the fair issue of his war upon Rome. He was the God of Enterprise, Commerce, and Travel, and was known to the Greeks as the 'Tyrian Hercules'‡—a name which contributed largely to the growth of the legends concerning their own Hercules. Traces of his worship, or at any rate of his worshippers, may be found in the

---

* *E.g.*, Hannibal (Grace of Baal), Hasdrubal (whose help is Baal), Maherbal, Adherbal, Mastanabal.

† *I.e.*, Melech Kirjath, 'King of the city.' Hence the names Hamilcar, Bomilcar, Himilco.

‡ Hercules, or the Greek form Heracles, was perhaps derived from the Phœnician title *Archal*, applied to Melcarth.

2—2

traditions of Elis and Olympia, where also was the statue of another deity of unmistakably Phœnician origin— Zeus Apomyius, he that wards off flies. At Sparta the festival of the Hyacinthia was more than possibly derived from the cult of Adonai; at Agrigentum was a temple to Zeus Atabyrius, a title purely Phœnician.*

Something has already been said of the arts of the Phœnicians. Those arts all flourished amongst the Carthaginians, as they had flourished in their earlier home. But there was one invention passed on by the early Phœnicians to the Greeks on which depends the whole place of that people in the history of civilization. This was the art of writing, the symbols of which, whether derived ultimately from Egypt or from Chaldæa, were brought by the merchants of Tyre to Thebes, and were thence called, in their earliest form, the Cadmean Alphabet.† With few alterations that alphabet has remained universal for the Western world.

Of the literature of Carthage there are no remains. When Rome took the town the whole of the voluminous libraries there found were handed over to the native princes of Africa, in whose hands they gradually melted away. One Mago had, however, composed a lengthy treatise on husbandry, which was so excellent, at least in its precepts, that it was translated into Latin by order of the Senate, and became a standard book on the subject even for the Romans. What its style may have been there is nothing to show us. There remain also two transcriptions of the records of Carthaginian explorers. The first, the Periplus of Hanno, relates how that admiral coasted southward from the Pillars of Hercules, carrying with him a crowd of colonists, whom he planted on the Moorish coasts. Then, sailing still southward, he tells how he saw the Fiery Mountain, supposed to have been the Cameroons Volcano, and the hairy apes, whom he named gorillas. The narrative was inscribed and

---

* Atabyris was the name of the chief mountain of Rhodes, and is Græcised from the Phœnician *Tabor*.

† Cadmus, the mythological founder of Grecian Thebes, is connected in name with Phœnician *Cadmon*, 'the Ancient One.' Thebes itself preserves the name of the older Egyptian Thebes, and its connection with Egypt seems to have been considerable.

dedicated in a Carthaginian temple, whence it was copied and translated by an unknown Greek. The other translation, a rendering in Latin verse by Festus Avienus of a similar voyage to the Northern seas, now goes by the name of the Ora Maritima. It is only a fragment, but it speaks of the Scilly Isles, and the ' Holy Island ' (Ireland), and the ' broad island ' of Albion. Beyond a few inscriptions dug up on the site of Carthage, there is no vestige to-day of what must once have been the language of a varied literature.

In the year 146 B.C. Carthage was besieged and sacked by the Romans, who had already disarmed it with what was truly ' *Perfidia plus quam Punica.*' For seventeen days its ruins burned, and then the remnant of its buildings were rased, and the site sown with salt. Modern excavations have brought to light something of the ancient plan of the city, some beautiful tessellated pavements, and a few other relics of the once mighty Queen of the West. But all that remains now are the broken basins of the Cothon and the Mercantile Harbour and a series of enormous cisterns, eighteen in number, each measuring one hundred feet in length by thirty in breadth, which formed the reservoir of the ancient city. Flames could not destroy them, so they were left—stones that cry out against the savagery of Roman vengeance. And the soil that covers the ancient site is built up of those many-coloured marbles which once decorated the temples and palaces of Carthage.

CHAPTER II.

Sicily and the Greeks.

Dimensions of the Island — Mountain System — Plains — Rivers — Fertility—Native Tribes ; Elymi—Sicels and Sicani—The Greek Colonies—Mistaken Policy of Carthage—Topography of Syracuse— Its Strength—Agrigentum and Gela—Selinus and Himera—Messana and other Ionic Towns—Remaining Hellenic Towns—The Carthaginian Reservation—Motye and Lilybæum—Magna Græcia—Preponderance of Achæans—Relationship of Colonies to their Mother-Cities—The Law-givers—Art and Commerce—Relations with Rome and Italy—Remains.

THE island of Sicily, the last remains of the belt of land which once joined Italy to Cape Bon, is a continuation of the mountain chain which descends through the length of Italy under the name of the Apennines. From the centre of the island to the north of the ancient town of Henna, three mountain ranges branch off, each running to one or other of the three capes which form the angles of a rude isosceles triangle. The apex of the triangle is Cape Drepanum in the west, and its base is the rough coast-line on the east between Cape Pelorus, the nearest point to Italy, and Cape Pachynus, the southernmost point of the island. The length of this base-line is approximately 115 miles; that of the two remaining sides 175 miles each. The total circumference is thus not more than 475 miles, and the area about 10,000 square miles, little more than one-sixth of the united area of England and Wales.

The whole of the interior region is ruggedly mountainous, and from the central ridges lesser spurs run down everywhere towards the coast. The eastern ridge, known as the Nebrodes Montes, rises at once from the northern shore, along which it lies for more than half of the entire length of the island. It is then met by the south-eastern ridge, and the area contained within the two is filled up by a labyrinth of precipitous valleys and steep hills, which gradually increase in height until they reach their maximum in the volcanic cone of Ætna, more than 10,000 feet above sea-level. Westward the actual ridge is less marked, but the whole region becomes one broken plateau difficult to traverse, except on foot. The central and southern mountains bore the name of the Heræi Montes.

What small area of plain the island contains lies along the coast, from Cape Passaro to Cape Grantola. At each of these points the mountains advance to the sea, and two lesser ridges intervene to divide the plain into three sections. The central area is that of Agrigentum, east-ward of which lies the Plain of Gela and Camarina, and westward that of Selinus. On the east coast the country opens into a smaller plain to the south of Syracuse. The nature of the country may best be understood from the fact that only two railways have been constructed across the interior. One leaving the coast at Catania (*Catana*) runs up to the centre of the island, passes through a valley which marks the juncture of the mountain systems, and, turning to the south, reaches the coast a little east of Girgenti (*Agrigentum*). The other starts from the last-named town, and runs straight across to the northern coast at Termini. In ancient times, too, these formed the only internal routes; the road which skirts the whole coast of the island has always been the chief means of communication.

Navigable rivers there are none, owing to the shortness of their courses; and of the few streams which deserve the name of rivers most are mere mountain torrents, flooded in times of rain, and dried up during the summer months. The most important stream is the Halycus (*Platana*), which rises in the centre of the island, and flows south-westward to the sea at Heraclea Minoa. Close to its source, but on opposite sides of the watershed, rise two streams, both called Himera. The smaller, falling into the northern sea by the town of the same name, forms, with the Halycus, the long valley through which runs the

Girgenti railway, and thus marks a natural boundary between the eastern and western portion of the island. The larger stream flows southward, and forms the boundary between Agrigentum and Gela. On the east coast the Symæthus, rising from numerous sources in the Nebrodes Montes, curves round the western base of Ætna and debouches between Catana and Leontini; and the Anapus, only worthy of mention as the river of Syracuse, falls into the great harbour, forming pestilent marshes about its mouth. Innumerable smaller streams enter the sea at every part of the coast, but few of them deserve the name of rivers. They serve, however, to impart to the soil that fertility for which it has always been famous. The land still yields wonderful harvests, though ill-cultivated. In older times the plains were the granary of Rome. Figs, olives, grapes, pomegranates, and fruits of every kind, flourished in the lowlands, so that *Geloi Campi*—a plain such as that of Gela—was a proverb for luxuriance. The marshy ground near the streams gave pasturage to the finest war-horses, and to racers that could vie with the 'mares of Elis.' And higher up in the highland valleys the groves of oranges and citrons flourish to this day upon the rich débris of volcanic mud and ashes.

When the first Greek settlers landed in Sicily, about the middle of the eighth century B.C., it was occupied by two races, the Sicels* and the Sicani. The former extended over the whole of the eastern half of the island as far as Henna; the latter possessed the western portion, with the exception of some half-dozen townships at the extreme north-west, where Egesta and Eryx were occupied by nondescript people called Elymi, who claimed to be descendants of the Trojans; while the Phœnicians possessed three great emporiums at Soloeis, Panormus,† and Motye. Who the Sicels and Sicani actually were, whence they came, and whether they were really one people, were questions debated even amongst the Greeks. It is probable that both emigrated from Italy, and were akin to the Sabellian and Oscan tribe known to the

---

* In Greek Σικελοι, of which Siculi is the Latin form.
† In Latin form Soloeis becomes Solus. Panormus is the modern Palermo, now the most important town in Sicily.

Romans as Lucani, Bruttii, Apuli, Campani, or Samnites. They probably supplanted a still older race, akin to the Messapians and Iapygians, who still maintained themselves in the heel of Italy, in Calabria, and whose remnant were the so-called Elymi. At any rate, they were not a commercial people, any more than were their Italian confrères, and so they permitted the settlement of the Phœnician traders at many points about the coast besides the great north-western marts, as, for example, at Megara Hyblæa and Ortygia on the east, Macara (afterwards Heraclea Minoa) on the southern shore. They confined themselves to agriculture, the produce of which they bartered with the Phœnicians ; and their religion was the worship of nature-powers personifying the mighty volcanic forces which shook the island. Their chief God was Adranus, whose sanctuary was Adranum, at the western foot of Ætna; their great Goddess Hybla gave her name to a number of townships, and to their own chieftains.* Other deities, called Palici, had their shrine amongst the Heræan hills; and most of the strong positions in which the highlands of the interior abound were crowned by Sicel or Sican fortresses. Such were Abacænum, in the north-east; Inessa, Centoripe, Bricinniæ, and Acræ, in the east and south; Agyrium, Assorus, and Henna, in the central region; and Entella, Schera, and Hercte, in the west.

Reports of the wonderful fertility of the island and the western shores of the Mediterranean reached Greece at a time when the older cities were rapidly rising in wealth and numbers, and seeking for new land in which to plant their surplus population. Already, before the eighth century B.C., the Æolians of Asia Minor had sailed into the far west, and the colony of Cumæ, on the coast of Campania, was of an immemorial antiquity. One Colæus, a Samian merchant, driven by storms out of his course, had been carried even to the Spanish Tartessus, where he realized such enormous profits from his cargo as to inflame the cupidity of all mercantile Greeks. In the year 735 B.C., the first colony was planted in Sicily by

* Hyblæa Geleatis, Hyblæa Heræa, Megara Hyblæa, and the surname Hyblon.

Thucles, who led a band of settlers from the Eubœan Chalcis and from Naxos, one of the most powerful of the Cyclades. He named his colony Naxos, after that island. In the next year, Archias of Corinth, one of the Bacchiadæ, the leading oligarchic family of that city, founded Syracuse (734 B.C.), driving out the Sicels, and perhaps the Phœnicians, too, from Ortygia, the small islet which formed his first settlement. Three years later the Naxians, under Thucles, colonized Leontini and Catana. In 730 B.C., arrived Lamis, from Megara, and, assisted by the Syracusans and Naxians, established himself at Trotilus. But the Sicels, grown jealous of the new-comers, drove him from that settlement, and even from a second position at Thapsus, a few miles north of Syracuse. Finally their chief, Hyblon, came to terms with the invaders, and allowed them to found a new Megara, surnamed Hyblæa, on the bay between Thapsus and Leontini.

A pause followed in the tide of immigration, during which the Hellenes perhaps waited to see the result of these first experiments. The rapid growth of the new colonies soon proved the feasibility of fresh attempts, and in 690 B.C. a body of Rhodians and Cretans founded Lindii, on the mouth of the little river Gela, in the most fertile region of all Sicily. The name was afterwards changed to Gela, and the town became the rival of Syracuse. The latter town was in a few years able to send out, on its own account, colonists who occupied Acræ, 664 B.C., and Casmenæ, 644 B.C. Its neighbour, Megara Hyblæa, was strong enough in another fifteen years to send out settlers to Selinus, on the very borders of Motye, 630 B.C., and in 599 B.C. the Syracusans founded a third colony at Camarina. In 582 B.C. the Geloans set the foundations of Agrigentum, whose magnificence was soon to eclipse even that of Syracuse. The date of the colonisation of Zancle (*Messana*) is uncertain, but probably comes about 650 B.C., when a band of Phocæan pirates seized it, and sent out thence, about a hundred years later, the colonists who occupied Himera.

Such was the map of Sicily about the middle of the

sixth century B.C. Within two hundred years the island had virtually passed from the hands of the Phœnicians to those of the Greeks. It was not the habit of the Phœnicians to build cities where they came. They were content to have harbourage and a market only. Hence the ease with which the Greeks supplanted them, the more as Carthage did not as yet see the need of constituting herself the champion of the Phœnician race. Decisive action might have prevented for ever the Hellenizing of the island ; but the opportunity was lost, and when at last she saw fit to dispute by force of arms the possession of what she had lost, Carthage found her rivals securely settled in walled cities, numerous, wealthy, and, moreover, little afraid of a nation which had so readily yielded to their stealthy inroads.

It remains to speak in detail of the principal Grecian cities, for the history of Sicily is little more than the history of a very few Hellenic towns, and of none have we anything like a continuous history save Syracuse. That colony was planted originally on the islet of Ortygia ('Quail Island'), which forms the northern horn of the bay, afterwards known as the Great Harbour. The opposite horn is formed by the promontory of Plemmyrium, and the river Anapus, falling into the Great Harbour, makes marshes and pools about its inner shores. Inland lies the small plain of Syracuse, through which flow the streams of the Cacyparis, Abolla, and Helorus ; and the coast road from Ortygia to the south, crossing this plain, was called, from the last-named river, the Helorine Way. The mountains, within whose curving line the plain is enclosed, reach almost to the sea on the northern side of the Anapus, sloping gradually down from the height called Euryalus to the flat ground immediately adjoining Ortygia. The slope, known as Epipolæ, breaks off on the north and south in steep scarps, and the level ground below was the site of the actual city of Syracuse when Ortygia had become too small for its growing population. In the times of Gelo it extended so much as to cover the whole seaward portion of the headland lying between the harbour and the Bay of Thapsus.

This was the region known as Achradina. Later it comprised two additional suburbs, Tyche on the northern angle, Neapolis at the southern corner towards the Helorine Way. Finally, when at her greatest size and power under Dionysius I., Syracuse spread even to the Epipolæ, which was enclosed, like the other regions of the city, in a continuous wall. Between the southern wall of Achradina and the islet lay an open space given up to tombs and called the Necropolis; and the narrow isthmus which joined Ortygia to the mainland formed the inner side of the Little Harbour (*Laccius*).

By nature the site of Syracuse was made to be that of the greatest city of Sicily. Protected by sea and marsh and mountains, it became, by the addition of walls, a place of immense strength; while Ortygia was a fortress absolutely impregnable by assault. It commanded the whole situation from the seaward side, harbours and streets alike; and the fortress of Euryalus, on the brow of Epipolæ, on the other side, was scarcely less difficult to assail, and equally commanding in its position. Of the other cities we have no such accurate topographical knowledge. Agrigentum was situated in a strong position by the shore, Gela on a less formidable site. Both derived their power and wealth from their admirable harbourage—that of Agrigentum being the better roadstead of the two—and from their command of the lowlands about them. The former city is described in another part of this book.* The Greeks knew it as Acragas, 'The Rocky,' and its site is still occupied by the small town of Girgenti. Gela is now Terra Nuova; and both have lost all their magnificence, and even the healthiness which must once have been theirs has disappeared with the decrease of cultivation. Syracuse, on the other hand, is still renowned for its climate and salubrity.

Selinus and Himera, the one on the southern, the other on the northern shore, stood as the bulwarks of Grecian Sicily against the Carthaginians and Elymi. The latter is the modern village of Bonformello, the former a heap

* See p. 88.

of unhealthy ruins still retaining the name of Selinunte. It stood on a narrow strip of land between the streams of the Hypsas on the east and the Selinus on the west, the upper waters of which rise near those of the famous Crimesus. Selinus, despite its late foundation, surpassed in magnificence most, if not all, of the Sicilian cities of its time, if one may judge from the ruins still remaining, and flourished long after its metropolis had utterly disappeared. The prosperity was doubtless due to the trade with the neighbouring Carthaginians, which fell naturally into the hands of the nearest city. To such a degree was this the case, that Selinus was regarded as half Carthaginian, and was chosen as a home by exiles banished from Carthage herself.

Messana, commanding the straits of the same name, survives as Messina, still an important town. Its original name was Zancle—'The Sickle'—from the curved form of the bay on which it stood. Opposite to it lay Rhegium —'The Rift'—whose name commemorated the volcanic convulsion which had riven Sicily from the mainland of Italy. The two cities were deadly foes, though both Ionic in their origin, owing to their jealousy of the trade which each wished to monopolize. This town, with Leontini (*Lentini*), Catana (*Catania*), and Naxos (afterwards Tauromenium, now *Taormina*), and Himera, formed the only Ionic cities of importance in Sicily, all others being essentially Doric; there were no Æolian or Achæan colonies in the island. Thermæ (*Termini*) and Cephalœdium (*Cefalu*) were smaller offshoots of Himera, respectively a little to the westward and eastward of that town; Acræ and Casmenæ were military outposts of Syracuse against the Sicels of the interior and the Greeks of the south-west coast respectively. Their modern names are Acremonte and Spaccoforno. Casmenæ and Camarina (*Camarana*) alike commanded the coast-road, which accounts for the early importance of the latter town and for the endless struggles between its more powerful neighbours for its possession. There were few Greek settlers in the interior, but Morgantia (now *Monte-Judica*), thirty miles west of Catana, and Henna (*Castro*

Giovanni) were gradually occupied by Hellenes until they lost their native Sicel character; and the same applies in the time of Dionysius' dynasty to many other Sicel towns. Tyndaris (*Tyndare*), a few miles west of Messana, was founded by the elder Dionysius 396 B.C., and became a town of some importance.

It will be noticed that all the chief Hellenic colonies were situate on the eastern or southern shores of the island. The absence of plains near the coast debarred the early settlers from frequenting the northern shore, and when in later days they made attempts to settle there, they were usually prevented by the hostility of the native tribes. But in the north-west and west the three great Phœnician marts maintained a long prosperity, only interrupted in the case of Motye. That town, situate at the point of Sicily nearest to Africa, was built on an island exactly similar to Ortygia, and was made a position of immense strength by artificial means. After its capture by Dionysius I., 397 B.C., it gradually sank in importance, and its place was taken by Lilybæum, a mile or so further south, whose harbour was at once the safest in Sicily and the most difficult of access, owing to the shoals and sandbanks at its mouth. It was famous in later times for its resistance to the Romans, but nothing is now left of it, and its site is marked by the small town of Marsala. Panormus and Drepanum, a lesser mart, still remain as Palermo, now the mart of Sicily *par excellence*, and Trapani. Solus, least of the three Phœnician settlements, a few miles west of Thermæ and Himera, early sank into decay.

The same stream of colonization which planted the Greeks in Sicily also fringed the shores of Southern Italy with Grecian towns, whose power and influence soon so far ousted the original inhabitants, and so far surpassed in importance Hellas proper, as to win for that region the name of Magna Græcia. Its limits were Tarentum on the east, and Posidonia (Pæstum) on the west, though this does not include the few Greek cities of Campania—Cumæ, Neapolis, and Dicæarchia. Here, too, the Achæan element was largely preponderant; but the Dorians and the Æolians, unrepresented in Sicily, had also considerable influence about the Gulf of Tarentum. The principal colonies of the Dorians were Tarentum, founded 707 B.C., by the so-called Epeunactæ and Partheniæ, said to be bastard Spartans expelled from Laconia at the close of the second Messenian war, and Heraclea. The Ionians colonized Siris and Elea. Locri Epizephyrii was a colony of Æolian outlaws, founded about 683 B.C., and famous afterwards as the ally of the Dionysian dynasty in Italy. The Achæans, however, occupied both the most numerous and the most advantageous sites. Sybaris (720 B.C.) and Crotona (710 B.C.), with their colonies Caulonia and Scylacium, Metapontum, Hipponium, Laus, Posidonium, and Thurii, were all colonies from Achæa. Sybaris, proverbial for its luxurious effeminacy, was rased by Crotona two hundred years after the foundation of the latter city. Posidonium still testifies by its ruins to the wealth and magnificence of its populace. The remnant of the Sybarites, assisted by colonists from all Greece, founded Thurii, near the ancient site of Sybaris, 443 B.C. Many Athenians joined in the enterprise, amongst them the historian Herodotus and the orator Lysias; and the town soon became the most important of the Lucanian Peninsula.

Though so far removed from their original homes, the colonists of Grecian towns never forgot their relationship to their metropolis, which they regarded as a child regards its parent. The leader of the colony was a citizen of mark and means, purposely chosen for the duty, and his memory was usually kept alive by heroic honours. The prytaneum (town-hall) of the colony contained the sacred hearth supplied by unfailing fires from that of the mother-city; the gods, customs, laws, and government of the mother-city were alike transplanted to the new settlement. This explains the tendency to oligarchic constitutions inherent in the mass of the Sicilian towns, descended as they were from Dorian parents. Troubles of course arose, as they always did amongst the restless Greeks; but frequently the attempt was made to arrange difficulties by an appeal to one citizen, who thus became nomothet, or lawgiver, to his countrymen. At Catana we hear of Charondas, 500 B.C.; at Locri, of Zaleucus about 660 B.C.; at Syracuse itself, of Diocles in 510 B.C., and eighty years later of Cephalus and Dionysius.

As with government and religion, so with art. The Sicilians maintained the traditions of their forefathers in their architecture, sculpture, and literature. The ruins of Selinus are those of three enormous temples, whose sculptured metopes bear the closest relation to the early work of the school which flourished in Ægina before the days of Athenian pre-eminence; the emulation of Syracuse, Gela, Agrigentum, and even of Camarina, brought from Olympia, and other national festivals, many a trophy; and the literature of the island can boast the perfection of comedy prior to the Athenians, the perfection of rhetoric before that became a recognised branch of study in Athens. For all this, Sicilian Hellenism was peculiar in many ways. Its constant intercourse with Africa and Italy brought into use many words which are unknown to Eastern Greece;* and, on the other hand, the Græcisms which occur in Latin are mostly due to the influence of Sicily.† The coinage of Syracuse and Rome was adapted to one common standard alien to Greece proper. The wide sea which lay between Greece and Sicily—wide to the navigators of those days, who deemed a straight course from Corcyra to Syracuse a venturesome thing—necessitated some differentiation between the two countries. And this was extended by the commerce of Sicily, which lay mainly in the western waters. They traded to Ostia, the port of Rome, for unwrought copper, to Etruria for wrought metals, to Africa and the Carthaginian ports to exchange their corn, wine and oil for the linen and purple and wrought fabrics of the Phœnicians.

Of all this manifold activity and wonderful prosperity, a prosperity whose vitality defied the oppressions of despotism and the sword of Carthage, little remains. At Selinus there still stands, or stood, one column of the

---

* *E.g.*, the names of the Roman divisions of the *as*, triens, tetrans, etc.
† *E.g.*, Æsculapius, Latona, machina; nummus, litra, hemina.

temple of Posidon and the Tyndaridæ ; at Agrigentum are the ruins of aqueducts and of the great temple of Zeus Atabyrius, which Phalaris commenced, and which was not finished until after the days of Thero. At Syracuse may still be seen some columns of the Olympieum by the Anapus, the theatre, aqueducts and conduits, and the quarries in which perished the remnant of Nicias' armament. But most of the remains are either purely or in part Roman, and the Sicily of the Greeks is recorded only in the pages of historians and poets.*

* Peculiar archæological value attaches to the coinage of the Sicilian cities, which are the best guides to their religion and customs, often to their history. The Sicilian coins are not only exceptionally numerous, but they are executed with a degree of art which makes them a class apart. The despots employed the best artists to produce the die, whose names were often added in tiny characters. The coinage of Magna Græcia approaches that of Sicily in its beauty, but that of Greece proper is far inferior in every way.

CHAPTER III.

The Gelonian Supremacy—Gelo.

Preponderance of Dorians in Sicily—Meaning of the Term 'Tyrannis '—
Its Development from Oligarchy—The Age of Tyrants—Causes of
the Permanence of Despotism in Sicily—Phalaris—Dorieus attempts
to colonise Eryx—Heraclea Minoa—The Despots of Gela ; Cleomenes
—Hippocrates—Gelo—His Origin—He seizes the Despotism, and
captures Syracuse—His Enlargement of the City—Great Power—
History of Messana—The Sam'ans—Invasion of Xerxes—The
Greeks appeal to Gelo—He refuses — His Reason — Battle of
Himera—Its Value—His Further Conquests, and Death—State of
Syracuse.

THROUGHOUT the history of Grecian Sicily the Dorian
element is always in the ascendant. Syracuse and Gela,
both direct Dorian colonies, and Agrigentum, an offshoot
of Gela, divided between them the hegemony of the
island ; and the less powerful sections of the Hellenic
peoples, Ionians and Achæans, and the native Sicel
states, and even the lesser Dorian cities, so far from ever
rivalling the pretensions of the great Dorian cities, have
actually no history of their own. They appear only as
prizes to be fought over by the Dorians of Sicily, or by
the Greeks of Hellas at large. Egesta and Leontini,
Messana and Camarina, in turn appear as *casus belli*,
and their continual seizure by one or other of the great
States, or by the Carthaginians, prevented their ever at-
taining to an importance of their own.

The inherent antagonism of Dorian, Ionian, and
Achæan Greeks, while it still remained a powerful
political factor, was nevertheless subordinated in Sicily
to the self-interest of the individual in a manner unknown

in historical Greece. Not only were Syracuse, Gela, and Agrigentum bitterly jealous each of the other, but it was a peculiarity of Sicilian Hellenism that, throughout its history, state jealousies should centre in the person of one individual. Thus the history of Sicily is the record of the endeavours of individuals to secure personal aggrandisement—the history of despots or tyrants.

By the term *tyrant* was meant, in Greece, one who put himself above the laws, refusing to be bound by them, while enforcing them at pleasure upon others. *Tyrannis* corresponds to the modern English phrase 'unlimited monarchy,' and just as an unlimited monarchy may be good and equitable, or the reverse, so the Greek tyranny was not necessarily oppressive and unjust. The associations which are connected in our minds with the word 'tyrant' are not essential features of the *tyrannos*, although, unfortunately, the great majority of Grecian despots confirm only too well the evil reputation of autocracy. Nevertheless, one of the most famous of the despots of Sicily, Gelo of Syracuse, left behind him so fair a name that when the island was 'liberated,' and the records of the tyrannies destroyed by Timoleon, popular feeling compelled him to spare the spot where the bones of Gelo were buried, and where his spirit was worshipped as that of a hero.*

That tyranny should at some time or other arise in every Greek community was a recognised step in their development. Originally governed by kings, they passed gradually under the power of a council of nobles, who encroached upon the royal authority until they entirely replaced it. These constituted the oligarchic governments, the second stage in political evolution. At first governing mildly and well, they came usually in course of time to abuse their power, and to exercise it for selfish ends alone. The mass of the people submitted perforce to the few in whose hands lay all the instruments of authority, physical and moral, until their very distress gained for them a champion. Sometimes he was one of

* A demigod—something more than merely human, but less than an actual God.

themselves; more often one of the oligarchs, grown dissatisfied with his fellows. In either case, by profuse promises, by inflammatory speeches, by professed sympathy—the recognised weapons of the demagogue, or popular leader—he secured the support of the multitude, and overthrew their oppressors, only to take up in his single person the despotic position lately occupied by an oligarchy which numbered perhaps several thousands. Having attained his aims by aid of the masses, he now turned against them and constituted himself *tyrannos*. His government was the third stage. It might endure but for his own lifetime. It might be handed down from father to son even for a hundred years. But sooner or later it fell before a new rising of the people, who took the government into their own hands and constituted a republic or democracy.

Through these stages passed, with the exception of Sparta, all the leading States of Greece. At Corinth, Sicyon, Argos, and Athens, in the Greek colonies on the coast of Asia, everywhere where Greeks came, the regular cycle was evolved. The period between 750-500 B.C. saw the *tyrannis* rise and fall in almost every community of Hellas proper, with a simultaneity which has secured for it the name of the Age of the Tyrants. And once overthrown, the tyranny rarely reappeared in Greece. But in Sicily the case was different. Arising about the same period as elsewhere, the Sicilian despots were able to reassert themselves despite all opposition until the last days of Grecian Sicily. When the island passed under the Romans, 241 B.C. Syracuse was still, as of old, under the dominion of a tyrant.

The causes of the continuance of the despotism in Sicily were various. The original settlers in each colony formed a close oligarchy of aristocrats, who viewed with dislike all encroachments upon their privileges, and thus, by their intolerance, left an unfailing handle to the attacks of self-seeking demagogues. Their power was strengthened by the fact that, as the wealthy class, they maintained the 'invincible cavalry,' for which Sicily was ever famous, and which gave them an immense advantage in point of force. Moreover, the indelible jealousies of State towards State, apart from the ever-present dread of Carthaginian attack, kept all in a condition of constant warfare, the condition most favourable for any one man's concentrating in his own person the power and respect of his fellow-citizens. It will be seen hereafter how often and how easily the peril of his State was the despot's opportunity. Something must be set down, too, to the diminutive proportions of even the most important States, which exposed them to such sudden and disastrous onslaughts as are unknown in the enormous States of to-day, and which could only be guarded against by a vigilance alien to the taste of a people engrossed as the Sicilians were in mercantile and agricultural pursuits. Lastly, the isolation of Sicily, its distance from the progressive mother country, the small influx of Hellenes from the older States now freed from despotism, and, not least, the continual contact with the Orientalism of the Carthaginians and Africa, induced a conservatism which strove to tolerate the original order of things—those oligarchies which were the hotbeds of despotism.

Most of these causes will be found to have been specially active at first in the western parts of the island, about Gela, Agrigentum, and Selinus, the farthest outpost of Hellenism in Sicily, and at Agrigentum accordingly we find the first recorded instance of despotism. Phalaris, one of the original settlers of Agrigentum, and an exile from Astypalæa in Rhodes, contrived to overpower his fellow-settlers and make himself despot of the town as early as 570 B.C., within fifteen years of its foundation. When entrusted with the building of a magnificent temple —and such magnificence was characteristic of the Sicilian towns—he collected a large number of artisans, whom he suddenly armed, and so mastered the place. It is possible that the citizens found it expedient to recognise as their leader one who was capable of holding in check the neighbouring Sicel tribes. We know that he warred against them with considerable success, and two hill-fortresses guarding the passage of the Himera, on the western side of Agrigentum, retained in their names the memory of the despot whose reputation for cruelty was imperishable.* He engaged one Perillus to construct a brazen bull, in which victims could be enclosed and roasted to death, and the most wholesome deed with which he is accredited is the burning of its inventor as the first experiment with this piece of ingenuity.† He maintained his position for sixteen years, being slain at the end of that period (circa B.C. 556) in a general rising under a noble named Telemachus. There is another, but improbable, story that he laid down his power voluntarily, with the remark that the people were like so many pigeons fleeing from a single hawk, whom, if they would but face, they were more than strong enough to destroy. In later times there was an attempt to re-establish his character, and in the so-called 'Letters of Phalaris'‡ he appears as a humane ruler, and the patron of literature and art.

Whether or no Phalaris was the first of the Sicilian despots, his example did not lack imitation. The close of the sixth century B.C. saw despots established at Zancle (Messana), Himera, Selinus, Gela, and Leontini, and we are justified in assuming that many, if not all, of the remaining cities suffered from the prevailing tendency to tyranny.

About 510 B.C.—the year of the expulsion of the Tarquins from Rome—Sybaris was rased by the Crotoniates, and there occurred the last attempt at colonization in Sicily by the mother country. It happened that Anaxandrides, one of the two kings of Sparta, having no children by his first wife, was ordered by the Ephors to marry a second, in the hope of preventing the extinction of the direct royal line. This second marriage resulted in the birth of a son, Cleomenes, who was thus heir to the kingship. Unhappily, however, the first wife shortly afterwards gave birth to three sons, Dorieus, Leonidas, and Cleombrotus. Dorieus, chagrined to find himself,

---

* See p. 148.

† He probably borrowed the idea from the human sacrifices offered to Moloch, who was represented by the Syrians as a bull.

‡ More famous than the *letters* is the dispute as to their authenticity, in which Dr. Bentley satisfactorily proved them a forgery—the work, probably, of some sophist. The story of his voluntary resignation probably arose at the same date.

though son of the legitimate queen, nevertheless subordinate to the earlier-born Cleomenes, determined to lead out a colony, and win a kingdom for himself. An attempt to settle at Cinyps in Libya was frustrated by the hostility of the natives and the Carthaginians, whose borders were threatened thereby; and after a three years' strife Dorieus was compelled to return to Sparta. Putting down his ill success to his not having consulted the oracles, he now sent to Delphi, and was ordered to colonize Heraclea. There was a legend that Eryx had been conquered by Heracles, and hither came Dorieus with a small force of Spartans. But the Carthaginians, relishing the advancement of Greek influence in western Sicily as little as in Libya, supported the native Sicels so successfully that the expedition was completely thwarted, and Dorieus himself slain. The survivors, under Euryleon, crossed to the southern coast, and there seized Minoa, the Selinuntine colony. Selinus was at the time under the despotism of Pithagoras. Euryleon united with the Selinuntines to expel the tyrant, and seized the despotism himself, only to perish in a speedy revolution. His followers, however, seem to have remained at Minoa, which was henceforth known as Heraclea Minoa.

It is about this time that the despots of Gela began to assert themselves in Sicily. Political division in that town had led to the expulsion of a body of the citizens who occupied Mactorium, an island town. Their return was effected by one Telines, himself a Geloan, apparently on the ground of religion; and in return for his services, in putting an end to domestic faction, he was invested with the hereditary priesthood of the Chthonian deities, whose commands he had obeyed. In the year 505 B.C. we find Cleander established as despot, so that the influence of Telines must very soon have failed. After a reign of seven years, Cleander was assassinated by a citizen, Sabyllus, but the power merely passed into the hands of his brother Hippocrates, 498 B.C. The new despot was an indefatigable soldier. He turned the mercenaries which his brother had levied against Greeks and Sicels alike; he reduced Naxos, and even Messana; then turned

eastward, and captured Leontini, and carried on a continuous war with the 'barbarians,' probably the western
Sicels and the Carthaginians. Finally, he attacked even
the Syracusans, and defeated them in a battle on the
Helorus. The latter appealed to Corinth and Corcyra
for arbitration, and a treaty was arranged, by which
their colony Camarina, which had already proved trouble-
some,* was surrendered to Gela, and the approach to
Syracuse herself thus thrown open. Hippocrates fell
about B.C. 491, before the walls of Hybla, where he was
engaged in battle with the Sicels, leaving two sons,
Euclides and Cleander.

His death was followed by an immediate rising of the
Geloans, who declined to acknowledge the authority of
his sons. The latter found, however, a pretended champion in their father's lieutenant Gelo, who brought up
his troops, routed the disaffected citizens, and finally,
setting aside the sons of Hippocrates, usurped the
tyranny for himself.

Gelo was descended from Telines, and therefore belonged to one of the principal families in the State ; for
the practice of a State priesthood in a Grecian community
implies at once large resources and wide influence. He
had enhanced this position by the brilliancy of his
services in the campaigns of Hippocrates, and was
probably high in favour with the mercenaries, the main
body of every despot's army. He was thus well qualified
to claim the position left vacant by Hippocrates, and he
justified his usurpation by the vigour of his actions. What
these were in detail we do not know, but they left him
free to turn to the best advantage the troubles which
shortly broke out at Syracuse. The aristocrats of that
State—the Gamori†, or land-owners—had made so bad
a use of their power as to provoke a coalition between
their own serfs—Cillicyrii—and the free populace, and

* Founded 599 ; it had disowned the authority of Syracuse as early as 550 B.C.
and had been reduced by force of arms.
† The *Gamori* were the descendants of the old settlers, the landed aristocracy.
The original inhabitants, whom they had disappropriated, became serfs bound to
the soil, and known as *Cillicyrii* (or *Cillyrii*). Between these two extremes lay
the mass of the people, independent, but landless, and mainly tenant-farmers or
petty traders.

were compelled to take refuge at Casmenæ. They invited the help of Gelo, who lost no time in coming to their support with so powerful a force that the newly-erected democracy surrendered themselves and their city unconditionally, 485 B.C.

But Gelo had no mind to take up arms merely to gratify the nobles of another State. He had recognised the incomparable advantages of Syracuse, whose soil and climate made it the peer of any situation in Sicily; while its position secured it from the aggressions of Carthage as far as might be, and brought it into close relations with the cities of Magna Græcia and with Central Hellas; and the islet of Ortygia, commanding alike the two harbours and the adjacent lowlands, marked it out as intended by Nature for the seat of a despot, who was bound by his very position to see an enemy in every man. Instead of restoring the city to its oligarchy, Gelo occupied it himself; and not content with the simple transfer of his residence thither from Gela, he proceeded to diminish the importance of the latter town by drawing off more than half its populace to Syracuse. Camarina he caused to be deserted, removing all its inhabitants in the same manner to Syracuse; and he even drew others from the neighbouring towns of Megara Hyblæa and Euboea, in both of which places the oligarchies resisted his usurpations, and were forced into migration. Strange to say, though it was the oligarchs who resisted him, he preferred to spare their lives on condition of their residing in Syracuse; while the mass of the populace, the demos, who had in no way opposed him, he expelled with an undeserved harshness, and even sold into slavery abroad. It was a maxim with him that 'a demos was a thankless thing to live with;' and, doubtless, it appeared more profitable to dismiss a population which had no other possession than its innate love of autonomy, and promised to contribute neither by its wealth nor its enterprise to the aggrandisement of the new capital of Sicily. For Syracuse now at once assumed this position—a position which it ever afterwards maintained. From the borders of Messana to those of Agrigentum, the whole of the Greek towns, with their fertile conterminous coastlands, were now under the yoke of Gelo. In the interior many of the Sicels paid him tribute, while beyond his own dominions he possessed a powerful ally in Thero of Agrigentum. Anaxilaus, despot of Messana and Rhegium, and Terillus, of Himera and Selinus, alone were neither in alliance with him nor in subjection ; while the latter town appears to have been a dependency of the Carthaginians.

The history of Messana about this period deserves a brief notice, as being one of the few minor Sicilian towns of which we have any detailed account. Under its original name of Zancle it had passed under the despotism of a citizen named Scythes, who was still in power when Hippocrates attacked it and reduced it to a dependency. Between Messana and Rhegium there had always been, as is natural with neighbours, a violent feud, arising probably from the attempt of each town to monopolize the command of the Strait of Messina. Shortly after the assault of Hippocrates news reached Sicily of the suppression of the revolt of the Ionian cities by Persia, 493 B.C., and the consequent exile of many of their former citizens. Amongst these were a number of Samians and Milesians, who, while casting about for a new home, received an invitation from their fellow-countrymen in Sicily to form there a new town at Cale Acte—Fair Head—a position on the north coast some miles west of Messana. With the exception of Himera, the north coast could boast as yet no Grecian settlements, and the Zanclæans undertook to establish the new-comers in the proposed position. Accordingly, the Samians and their fellow-fugitives crossed to Italy en route for Zancle, putting in at Locri on their way westward. Here they were visited by Anaxilaus, of Rhegium, who saw in them the means of crushing his rival on the opposite shore of the Strait. Scythes, he told them, was at the moment absent in the interior with the bulk of the armed force of the Zanclæans, and he advised them to seize the defenceless city for themselves. With inexcusable ingratitude they snatched at the idea, and occupied Zancle. Scythes, finding himself thus ejected, appealed to his over-lord Hippocrates, who replied by putting him under arrest for having permitted the loss of one of the Geloan vassal States, and forthwith marched northward to recover it himself. But the Samians persuaded him to an act of treachery as unwarrantable as their own, and he contented himself with seizing the persons and property of all the Zanclæans without the walls, leaving all within the walls in the hands of their captors. The whole of the ejected inhabitants thus became the prisoners of Hippocrates, who sold them into slavery. The Samians retained their ill-gotten gains but a little while, for they were in turn expelled by Anaxilaus, who thus constituted himself despot of that town as well as of Rhegium, and changed its name to Messana.

Now undisputed master of the greater part of Sicily, Gelo stepped forward as the champion of Hellenism against Barbarians, and undertook the expulsion of the Carthaginians and Elymi from their possessions in the west of the island.* How far he succeeded we do not know; but his partial success seems to be proved by the subsequent efforts of Carthage to retaliate, and by the appeal now made to him for assistance by the Hellenes of Central Greece.

In the year 480 B.C. Xerxes, the successor of Darius on the throne of Persia, crossed the Hellespont and marched overland through Thrace and Macedonia, to effect that conquest of Hellas which his father had ten years before failed to achieve, with an army estimated at more than 1,000,000 men, superbly appointed, and supported by a prodigious fleet. His approach threatened the extinction of Grecian nationality, and very many of the Hellenic States, notably Thebes, had already made their submission to him. But a small band of patriots gathered round Sparta and Athens and made what efforts they could to resist the impending storm while it was still distant; and, amongst other measures, they despatched to Syracuse a joint embassy of Spartans, Athe-

* Herod. vii. 158. He declared himself the avenger of Dorieus' death, and seems to have asked the aid of the Greeks of Central Hellas, which was refused.

nians, and Corinthians, to solicit the assistance of one who was then reputed the most powerful and wealthy of the Greeks. His available forces were numbered at 24,000 infantry and 4,000 horse, and a fleet of 200 ships of war; while he could provision the whole Greek army, it was said, for an indefinite period.

In the late autumn of 481 B.C. the embassy arrived at Syracuse. Gelo listened to their address with attention, and replied that he would put his whole force into requisition for the defence of Hellas, on the one condition that he should be recognised as the sole general of the Greeks. Such a proposal met with a hot refusal from the Spartans, who at that date, and for many years previously, laid claim to the hegemony of Hellas. Gelo then declared that he would be satisfied to be sole commander of half the Grecian forces, whether the land or sea armament. But while the Spartans again declined to surrender the command of the army, the Athenians now also refused to put themselves under the rule of Gelo as admiral. Whereupon the despot replied that they seemed to have commanders enough whatever their forces might be, and bade them return and tell their countrymen that 'their year had lost its spring,' implying that without his aid the efforts of Greece were likely to bear small fruit.

The above story comes to us from Herodotus, who probably drew somewhat on his imagination. The facts of the case seem to be that Gelo could not spare any help for his countrymen against their Eastern enemies, for he was at the moment threatened with an attack scarcely less formidable from a Western foe. Taking advantage of the troubles of Central Greece, and probably incited by Xerxes, whose fleet was mainly levied from the Phœnician dockyards, the Carthaginians were preparing a huge armament, which should sweep the Hellenes from Sicily, and avenge the recent aggressions of Gelo.

Their immediate opportunity arose from the expulsion of Terillus from Himera by Thero, despot of Agrigentum, at the invitation of the inhabitants of that town. Terillus put himself under the protection of Carthage, and his case was so energetically supported by his son-in-law, Anaxilaus, that in 480 B.C. Hamilcar, one of the *suffetes*, appeared on the west coast with an armament stated at 300,000, with a proportionate number of horses and chariots, and a fleet of 3,000 ships of war, besides transport vessels. Without delay he laid siege to Himera, whose inhabitants prepared for defence by blocking up the gates of their town, and awaiting the arrival of aid under Thero and Gelo. The latter is said to have brought with him 50,000 foot and 5,000 horse; and the Grecian army could hardly have numbered less than 60,000 in all. The battle which followed lasted throughout the whole of the day. Before its commencement Gelo intercepted a message announcing the approach of a body of horse from Selinus in support of Hamilcar. He at once despatched a squadron of his own cavalry, who impersonated the Selinuntine reinforcements, and so gained ingress to the Carthaginians' camp. Thereupon, throwing off their disguise, they put the whole host into such disorder that the simultaneous onslaught of the main body of the Grecian army was enabled, after a desperate resistance, to make good their advantage. The slaughter of the Carthaginians was immense—Gelo's victory complete. The broken remnants of the enemy —native Carthaginians and Libyans, Iberians from Spain and Ligyes from the region of the Maritime Alps, Sardinians, Corsicans, and other mercenaries from all parts of the Western Mediterranean basin—escaped as best they could; their general was never seen alive again. His actual fate remained an insoluble mystery. According to one account, he was slain in camp by the cavalry of Gelo; the Carthaginians declared that he threw himself into the flames in which he had throughout the day been sacrificing for the success of his arms. The triumph of Hellenism in Sicily was coincident with the still greater triumph of the Greeks at Salamis, when the united fleets of Central Hellas utterly destroyed the Persian fleet and saved Greece. Legend said that the battles of Himera and Salamis were fought on one and

the same day. Certain it is that the swarms of barbarians that threatened the Grecian race at the same
moment in the east and in the west were both driven
back at much the same date by forces immeasurably
inferior in everything but courage. The result of the
Xerxeian invasion did not, however, reach Gelo before
he had prudently despatched a confidential envoy named
Cadmus, the son of the above - mentioned Scythes of
Zancle, to Greece, there to watch the course of events,
and should the arms of Persia prevail, as seemed inevitable, to do homage to the invader on Gelo's behalf. The
event saved alike the name of Greece and the honour of
Gelo ; and the offerings which the Central Hellenes dedicated at Delphi in memory of their victory stood side
by side with others far more magnificent, recording the
triumph of their Sicilian brethren.*

The victory of Himera left Gelo in a position never
attained by any other Grecian despot. He was looked
up to as a hero and the saviour of his people. All Sicily
acknowledged his supremacy excepting the small western
corner where the Carthaginians still maintained their
footing. Whether he made any attempt to push his
successes further in that quarter we do not know, but we
are told that a peace was shortly after concluded with
Carthage, at the cost, to the latter State, of 2,000 talents
as an indemnity. But there is reason to believe that
patriotism has caused the historians of these events to
exaggerate the truth, for within a very few years the
Carthaginians once more assumed the aggressive—a
course which they were usually slow to follow after any
disastrous reverse. Himera, however, was saved and
handed over to Thrasydæus, son of Thero, and it may be
regarded as certain that Anaxilaus was forced to acknowledge the supremacy of Gelo, and that when the latter
died within a year of his success, he left to his successor
an undisputed sovereignty over all the Grecian States of
the island. He died of a dropsy, 479 B.C., the most
renowned of the Greeks of his day and the idol of

* The ruins of a large temple, erected in memory of the victory, at Himera,
were brought to light only recently.

the Syracusans, who raised to his memory a group of nine monumental columns, and abrogated in his favour the law which forbade expensive public funeral ceremonies, despite his deathbed wish that it should be adhered to in his case as in that of any meaner citizen. He was worshipped as a hero—as a being, that is, more than mortal if less than divine—and his name never faded from the grateful memory of his people. By his wife, Damarete, he left one son, still young; and his brothers, Hiero, Polyzelus, and Thrasybulus, all survived him.

In the short reign of Gelo as despot of Syracuse, that city attained the position, which it ever afterwards held, as mistress of Sicily. His efforts to aggrandize it had led to its rapid growth; and not only did he people it with enforced colonists, but many new settlers came thither from Greece—in part attracted by his fame, in part to escape the threatened dominion of Persia. Previous to 485 B.C. the whole town had been comprised within the small area of Ortygia; but at his decease it had spread to the large part of the adjacent mainland called Achradina. How large was the increase of the population may be inferred from the fact that he gave the citizenship to 10,000 of the mercenary troops which formed his standing army. Yet, despite the walls and arms by which he guarded his power, his rule was mild and paternal, rather that of a constitutional monarch than a despot; and the proof of this is the voluntary immigration of free Greeks to Syracuse, the absence of all those dark deeds which branded the memory of a Dionysius or an Agathocles, and that dying request by which he bade the people obey their laws in his burial. Simonides, the elegiac poet, who composed the dedicatory couplets upon his offerings at Delphi, spoke of him as one who 'conquered the nations of the Barbarians, and gave freedom to the Greeks with a mighty hand.'

CHAPTER IV.

Hiero.

Character of Hiero—He expels his Brother—Quarrels with Thero—Betrays Himera—Anaxilaus—Foundation of Ætna—War with Etruscans — Battle of Cumæ — Death of Thero — Thrasydæus makes war on Hiero—His expulsion—Micythus of Rhegium—Death of Hiero—His Olympic Victories, and Patronage of Literature.

BY the will of Gelo his power was divided between two of his brothers, of whom one, Polyzelus, obtained command of the army, while the other, Hiero, was appointed to the government of Syracuse. The latter was already known as something more than a despot's brother. As early as 488 B.C. he had gained an Olympian victory in the single horse race, and had continued to enter for the palm at Olympia, Delphi, and elsewhere, year after year. He was a man of violent and selfish ambition, and little likely to share his empire quietly with anyone. Moreover, he was brother-in-law alike of Anaxilaus and of Thero, and in every way a more prominent figure than was. Polyzelus. The latter was supported by Damarete, widow of Gelo and now wife of Polyzelus; and the quarrel between the brothers reached such a height that in 478 B.C. Damarete and her husband were forced to leave Syracuse, and appeal to the protection of Thero. That despot granted them an asylum at Agrigentum, but made no active efforts to restore them to Syracuse. Hiero at once demanded that they should be expelled from Thero's dominions, and marched upon Agrigentum, with the whole force of Syracuse, to enforce his demand. He had already reached the river Gela, the eastern boundary of the territories of Thero, when the poet Simonides contrived to bring about a reconciliation, and Hiero abandoned his purpose.

His quarrel with Thero had, however, induced the Himeræans to appeal to him for protection from the lawless despotism of Thrasydæus, son of Thero. Headed by two cousins, rivals of Thero, the disaffected party in Himera prepared to revolt so soon as Hiero should appear before their gates. But Hiero, besides disappointing them by his reconciliation with Thero, committed an act of positive treachery. He betrayed the names and plans of the malcontents, and so enabled Thrasydæus to anticipate their action, which he did with such severity that he found it necessary to recruit the numbers of the remaining populace by enforced immigration.

Meanwhile Hiero proceeded to quarrel with his other brother-in-law, Anaxilaus, who was meditating an advance upon the Locrians. The latter put themselves under the protection of Syracuse, and the threat of war was sufficient to restrain Anaxilaus, who had not yet forgotten the ill-success of his efforts to shake the power of Gelo. He consented to abandon his design, and so maintained his position in peace until his death, 476 B.C.

Thus balked a second time of an excuse for extending his power by force of arms, Hiero had recourse to scarcely less violent means. It was the summit of the ambition of a Greek of his day to become the *œcist*,* or founder of a new town. Such a position was equivalent to a title to such heroic honours as Gelo had attained by his repulse of the Carthaginians. But the foundation of a colony in the orthodox way was too tedious and speculative a method for Hiero. He expelled from Naxos and Catana their Greek inhabitants, left the former town desolate, and handed over its lands to be shared, together with those of Catana, by settlers of his own providing, who occupied the old town of Catana under the new name of Ætna, 476 B.C. These settlers, 5,000 from Greece, 5,000 mercenaries from Hiero's own guard, served as a bulwark to his power, seeing that their own position depended on the maintenance of their *œcist's* rule. Two

---

* Οἰκιστής, one who establishes an ἀποικία, or colony.

years later the despot carried off the prize, with a four-horse chariot, at the Pythian games, and was proclaimed before all Greece as Hiero the Ætnæan.

About the same time the Greeks of Cumæ, the oldest Hellenic colony of Italy, being harassed by the attacks of Etruscan privateers, appealed to Hiero for protection. Etruria, though at this time falling away from her former mighty power in Central Italy before the growing strength of Rome and the pressure of the Gauls, was still mistress of that portion of the Mediterranean waters to which she left her name—the Tyrrhene, Tuscan or Lower Sea, between the shores of Italy, Sicily, Spain, and Gaul. Her pirates, starting from the seaport of Pyrgi near Cære, ravaged the Campanian and Latian coasts, maintaining thieves' honour with the Phœnician buccaneers of Sardinia and Africa. The news that Hiero meditated asserting himself as the custodian of the seas, affecting as it did Phœnician and Etruscan interests alike, led to the appearance of a formidable combined fleet of those two nations off the Italian coasts. The fleet of Hiero engaged them off Cumæ, and gained a complete victory, and the spoils which the victor sent as offerings to the shrines of the Grecian Gods reached their destination about the same time as occurred his victory at Delphi. Amongst those spoils was the bronze helmet of an Etruscan warrior which was dedicated at Olympia, and was there found not many years ago, with the inscription recording its donor and the event—474 B.C.

In the next year died Thero, after governing Agrigentum for fifteen years with a rule so mild that his memory was honoured as that of a hero. Like Gelo, he set an example of the better side of tyranny ; like Gelo, he laboured to beautify and enrich his capital, of which the chief ruins are those of temples raised by him ; and like Gelo, he won a Hellenic fame as an Olympian victor and the partner of Gelo's triumph at Himera. But his death was speedily followed by trouble. His son Thrasydæus, who succeeded to the despotism, was already notorious for his excesses at Himera. He practised at Agrigentum the same cruelties, and in a mistaken moment provoked

Hiero to war. The latter forestalled attack by at once invading the territories of Agrigentum, where he met Thrasydæus' army, and routed it with a loss of four thousand men. So utterly was that despot's power broken that, unable to regain his authority, he fled to Megara on the Isthmus of Corinth, where he learnt how his late behaviour was regarded by the free Hellenes. The Megarians at once put him upon his trial as a tyrant, and executed him 472 B.C. The Agrigentines, thus rid of their master, made terms as best they could with Hiero, to whom we must suppose they owed at least a nominal obedience, together with the other Grecian cities of Sicily.

Even Messana and Rhegium must now have become acknowledged dependencies of Syracuse, for, about 470 B.C., Hiero dictated his wishes to the Rhegines and was at once obeyed. The late despot Anaxilaus had left the government in the hands of a trusted freeman, Micythus, in wardship for his own young children, Micythus governed so equitably that the Rhegines were well content to accept his dominion. But Hiero found here an opportunity for extending his influence, and presently ordered him to surrender the government to the rightful heirs, now grown up. Micythus did so at once, rendered exact account of his guardianship, and then retired to Tegea in Arcadia, where he lived as a private citizen. Hiero himself died 467 B.C. from a disease which had long invalided him. His fame rests as much on the odes of Pindar, and on the Olympian and other victories which they celebrate, as on his warlike exploits. Twice was he crowned victor in the single horse-race, and in the year before his death he attained the desired place of conqueror in the race of four-horsed chariots. When we remember the treatment of the expelled Thrasydæus by the Megarians, the anomaly of the position of other despots, such as Gelo, Thero, and Hiero, and in later days Dionysius I., becomes striking indeed. They were stigmatised as tyrants and *ipso facto* beyond the pale of law, and yet were allowed, could they deserve the honour, to be crowned with the olive of Olympia, the laurel of Delphi, or the parsley of

the Isthmian games.   In the case of Gelo and Thero there
was a gentleness of rule and a great deliverance from the
common foe to cloak their despotism ; but Hiero had no
such extenuating circumstances to plead, while his conduct was marked by avarice, violence, and espionage.
Nevertheless, he maintained, and even extended, the power
bequeathed to him by his brother ; and only after his
death could men see how much he had failed to consolidate it.   One merit he had which seems ill-consistent
with the general tone of his character—he was a muni-
ficent patron of literature.   Simonides and Bacchylides,
Epicharmus and Æschylus, either resided or visited at
his court ; and Pindar, the most famous lyric poet of
that or any century of Grecian life, found it in every way
worth his while to glorify the victories of Gelo, Hiero,
and Thero at the national festivals of Hellas ; and in
473 B.C. he personally visited the Syracusan court.
Such hospitality cost little to Hiero, while it secured him
the ' monument more enduring than bronze '—odes and
hymns superscribed with his name.

CHAPTER V.

Thrasybulus and the Liberation.

Tyranny of Thrasybulus—General Revolt of the Greeks of Sicily—
Blockade of Ortygia—Thrasybulus retires to Locri—Disestablish-
ment of the Gelonians—They seize Ortygia—Final Accommodation
— Restoration of Camarina — The Thousand at Agrigentum —
Petalism at Syracuse—Rise of Ducetius—His Surrender and Retirement to Corinth—His Return—Syracuse at War with Agrigentum
—Period of Peace—Progress—Peloponnesian War—Indifference of
the Sicilian Greeks—The Dorian Siceliots attack the Ionic Cities,
which appeal to Athens—Laches and Charœadas—Sophocles, Demosthenes, and Eurymedon —Sphacteria—The Fleet reaches Sicily too
late— Pacification of Gela — The Syracusans expel the Leontine
Democracy—Embassy of Phæax—The Leontine Oligarchs Appeal
to Athens, as do the Egestæans at War with Selinus—Athenian
Embassy to Egesta.

Two rivals now claimed the *tyrannis*, one the son of Gelo,
the other Thrasybulus, his uncle, the fourth and last of
the sons of Deinomenes.   The latter contrived to gain all
real power, and commenced a despotism of the very
worst kind, banishing and putting to death numbers of
the citizens in order to confiscate their property.   He
disgusted even the Gelonians, but contrived to retain the
favour of the mercenaries ; so that, when a general revolt
broke out in the year 467-66 B.C., he was able to rely
upon the settlers from Ætna, Hiero's mercenary colonists,
and to get together a force of some 15,000 in all, with
whom he could garrison and maintain Ortygia.   The
insurgent citizens occupied the rest of the town—Achradina as it was afterwards called*—within its own walls,
and from these two positions, as if from camps, the two

---

* Syracuse was not yet extended to Tyche, Neapolis, etc.

parties carried on their struggle. But to expel the despot from his stronghold by themselves was beyond the Syracusans; and they enlisted on their side the whole force of Sicily by declaring the Gelonian dynasty at an end, and inviting the Greeks to share in its final overthrow. From Agrigentum, Gela, and Himera, from Selinus, now once more independent, even from the Sicel tribes of the interior, came speedy reinforcements. The island rose as one man against the one individual who claimed the sceptre of Gelo ; and, shut up within his island-castle, he was forced to surrender. He was allowed to retire to Locri, a town always closely connected with the despots of Syracuse, and now repaying to Thrasybulus the debt incurred by Hiero's defence of it against Anaxilaus. There he lived as a private citizen until his death.

So fell the Gelonian dynasty (end of 467 B.C.), and with it for a time, before the rising tide of democracy, was swept away all similitude of *tyrannis* in the island. The strong hand of Hiero had prevented the rise of any despot of importance after the death of Thero, so that there was left no weighty obstacle to the popular movement, which seems to have been first seen in the expulsion of Thrasydæus, 473 B.C. For sixty years from this date Sicily remained free from despotism, and in that period is contained all that is glorious in her national history as a Grecian island.

The retirement of Thrasybulus did not, however, put an immediate stop to the difficulties of the Syracusans, who had now to deal with the whole remaining number of the Gelonian partisans, including the Hieronian settlers and the mercenaries of the late despot. All or most of these had been enriched by the grant of lands and goods wrung from expelled exiles; and now those exiles streamed back from all quarters, clamouring for the restitution of their citizen-rights and their property. Their momentary confidence and hatred for the defeated party led the new Government to pass a decree ordering the restoration of all illegally-acquired property, and prohibiting from office any one of Gelonian leanings. The natural result was a civil war, in which the new democracy of united Sicily was arrayed against the Ætnæans, the mercenaries, and doubtless large bodies of Gelonians recently expelled from the other Sicilian cities. The latter party again occupied Ortygia, and it was only by the institution of a regular blockade that they were at length driven out. The struggle in turn affected most of the cities of the island, and finally centred at Ætna, where the dispossessed Catanæans, supported by the Sicels under their chief Ducetius, succeeded at last in recovering their ancient home from the remnant of the Gelonians. They restored the name of Catana, overthrew the tomb and monuments of Hiero, while the fugitive Hieronians established themselves at Inessa, a Sicel town of the interior, which they renamed Ætna. Finally, the united Sicilians agreed to permit the occupation of lands at Messana and Camarina by the Gelonians, and this latter town, after having lain desolate for more than twenty years since Gelo had dismantled it, once more became a Hellenic city, 461 B.C., and it is surprising to find one of its new inhabitants proclaimed victor in the chariot-race at the Olympic games of 452 B.C.* This was Psaumis, to whose efforts the re-establishment of the town was largely due. For some little time longer the troubles went on, but they were no longer caused by the attacks of any hostile faction, but by the disturbances natural before the newly-created democracies could settle down into solidarity. At Agrigentum the first form of government was a limited democracy, controlled by a council of one thousand. But the tendency of the council to oligarchy, or even to despotism, led to a rising under the philosopher-poet Empedocles, and the subversal of the one thousand to give place to a complete democracy. At Syracuse, too, the pacification of the Gelonians was followed by so many efforts on the part of rich men to re-establish the *tyrannis* that a safeguard was introduced on the plan of the Athenian ostracism. By its means any citizen whose power threatened to endanger the State was open to a sort of impeachment. Every voter wrote upon an olive-leaf the name of the citizen whom he deemed dangerous,

* The most expensive ἀγών, and a sure sign of prosperity and wealth.

and the individual thus accounted the most formidable was constrained to go into exile, though only for five years. This Petalism* proved, however, so liable to abuse, sweeping away all well-to-do men who took part in politics, and thus intimidating others from following their example, that it was very shortly afterwards abolished, and the State slowly settled into rest and peace.

Meantime, the Sicel chief Ducetius, set free from the dominion of the Gelonian dynasty, began to aim at a wider sovereignty for himself. He formed a federation of the petty communities of the interior, and with the support thus given him, he took the fortress of Morgantine and founded Palice as the centre of his league. The town took its name from the *Palici*, Sicel Nature-Gods, there worshipped; and its reputed sanctity, no less than its central position, made it an admirable place for the capital of a native league.† Ducetius now set himself to avenge the diminished power of the Sicels on the Greeks. He stormed and recovered Inessa, which the Hieronians from Ætna had occupied, and in the year 452 B.C. was bold and strong enough to march down into the territories of Agrigentum, the second city of Sicily. There he laid siege to a small fortress called Motyum, and was fortunate enough to defeat a combined army of Agrigentines and Syracusans coming to its relief. But his success was shortlived. Unable to take Motyum, he was attacked by a second joint army, and so completely defeated that he left his own kingdom, rode into Syracuse, and there placed himself as a suppliant at an altar. Probably the ill-success of his siege operations had spread dissatisfaction amongst his mountain troops, to whom all long service would be irksome, particularly if not brilliantly successful. The Syracusans, despite the reluctance of Agrigentum, spared the suppliant's life, and sent him to Corinth, where they undertook to provide for his maintenance, while he gave his word of honour to attempt no return (451 B.C.).

Despite the threatening attitude of the Sicel federa-

---

* πεταλισμός, for πέταλον, leaf, from the leaf of olive used as a tablet. Cf. ὀστρακισμός, from ὄστρακον, oyster-shell.
† Compare with the history of Megalopolis and Arcadia.

tion, Syracuse had been able to send out fleets during the years 453—452 B.C. to suppress the piracy of the Etruscans. The death of Hiero had removed the hand which chastised them at Cumæ, and their buccaneering had doubtless thereupon broken out with fresh violence. But the fleet which had sailed under Hiero's orders was still as effective as ever under the democratic administration. Ilva (Elba), a famous iron-producing island, was ravaged 453 B.C., and in 452 B.C. Corsica was plundered, Ilva annexed, and the coasts of Etruria itself insulted by the Syracusan admiral Apelles.

In 448 B.C. (?) Ducetius broke his word, and presented himself once more in Sicily, where he succeeded in founding a town at Cale Acte, the site formerly selected by the Samian refugees.* His old subjects rejoined him in numbers, and the Agrigentines, disgusted to see him again a dangerous foe, and to find their opposition to the leniency of Syracuse thus amply justified, declared war upon that city. The war ended in the Agrigentines being forced to sue for peace ; but it gave Ducetius the opportunity of securing his new position. But his death, which followed soon after,† again broke up the Sicel league, and the Syracusans proceeded at leisure to reduce many of the towns of the interior (446 B.C.).

The twenty years succeeding the death of Ducetius seem to have been years of general peace. During this period the Sicilian cities grew to that opulence and magnificence for which they were afterwards famous. Their commerce increased enormously, particularly the export trade in wine and oil from the Southern coast to Africa, to which trade Agrigentum owed her proverbial riches. The overthrow of the despots and the development of free government, if it reduced the ranks of court poets, gave birth to the famous rhetoricians Gorgias of Leontini, Corax and Tisias at Syracuse, and the Agrigentine Polus, while Empedocles in Sicily won a name little inferior to that of the Eleatics in Italy—Parmenides and Zeno, the philosophers of Elea (Velia), near

---

* See p. 42.
† The date is uncertain ; probably earlier than 440 B.C.

Pæstum. The exponents of the fine arts in Sicily and Magna Græcia rivalled the descendants of Myron and Polygnotus in Central Greece, and the temples of Agrigentum were worthy that even the great Zeuxis should adorn them with his marvellous 'Lacinian Juno,' whose beauty was the combined beauty of the five fairest maidens in Agrigentum—and the beauties of Agrigentum are famous still. The coinages of Sicily had no rival for number and grace and workmanship.

In 431 B.C. broke out the Peloponnesian War. The small beginning of that twenty-seven years' struggle was a quarrel between Corinth, the mother-city of Syracuse, and Corcyra, another of her colonies. Corcyra appealed to Athens, and the latter power pledged herself to a defensive alliance with the Corcyræans, whose island position and formidable navy made them inevitably the rivals or the allies of Athens in the great war which everyone felt to be already 'in the air.' Not the least reason for the alliance was the knowledge that, should war break out, the Dorian cities of Sicily would at once be called upon for supplies, in which event Corcyra would be an invaluable station for intercepting the western fleets and convoys. The war broke out at once, precipitated by the very alliance which was intended to guard against it; and the expected requisition was issued by Sparta, as head of the anti-Athenian league, that the Sicilian Dorians should contribute their share to an enormous fleet of 500 triremes.

But secure and prosperous in their isolation, untouched by the aggressions of either Athenian or Lacedæmonian, and well aware that to meddle in another's quarrel brings little gain, the Sicilian Greeks were not eager to engage in so distant a war. Most of the Dorian cities of the south coast were already in a manner allied with Sparta, and some of the Chalcidian towns, such as Naxos, Catana, Leontini, and Rhegium in Italy, may have been in like manner allies now, and they certainly were shortly after, of Athens. But the alliance, when it existed, counted for little, and the Sicilians as a whole were content to watch the struggle for the hegemony of

Greece without committing themselves to anything more decided than a Dorian or Ionian sympathy with the belligerents.

But the certainty—so it was believed—of Athens' speedy fall incited the Dorians of Sicily to aggressions upon the few small Ionic and Chalcidic towns. Those towns, Naxos, Catana, and Leontini, lying between the important State of Messana and Syracuse herself, were ill prepared to resist. They found allies indeed in the Dorian Camarina, now grown afraid of the neighbouring power of Syracuse and Rhegium, which was, as always, at feud with the Locrians, the Italiot allies of Syracuse, and therefore sided with the anti-Syracusan minority. But these were as nothing to set against the forces of Syracuse, Gela, Agrigentum, Selinus and Messana. Accordingly, in 427 B.C., the rhetor Gorgias headed an embassy to Athens to entreat armed support. His trained eloquence found ample support in the dictates of prudence, which forbade Athens to permit the destruction of the only local check upon Dorism in Sicily. The success of their operations against the Ionic cities would naturally be followed by the active interference of the Dorians in Greece. Accordingly, a fleet of twenty triremes was despatched 427 B.C., under Laches and Charœades, to defend the Athenian allies in Sicily and to examine into the advisability of offensive action.

The arrival of this squadron found Naxos and her fellow-towns blockaded by land and sea. It took up its quarters at Rhegium, now an ally of Athens, and acted so vigorously about the straits that Messana gave hostages for its peacefulness, and the blockade was thus raised on the north side, 426 B.C. Laches, now left sole commander by the death of Charœades, seems to have exceeded his orders, for he now attacked Inessus, the Sicel town in the interior, which was held by a Syracusan garrison. The attack was repulsed with loss, and Laches returned to Rhegium, having concluded an alliance with the non-Hellenic town of Egesta, 425 B.C. At Rhegium he found his successor Pythodorus already arrived, and the precursor of a second and larger fleet of forty

vessels under Eurymedon and Sophocles, which was intended to arrive in the spring of that year. The news
of its approach spurred the Sicilian Dorians to greater
activity, and a combined squadron of Locrians and Syracusans succeeded in recovering Messana by the help of
some partisans within the walls. Then, massing their
fleet at that point to more than thirty sail, they made an
effort to crush the Athenian fleet in the harbour of
Rhegium before the reinforcement could come up. The
battle which followed ended in a complete victory for the
sixteen Athenian and eight Rhegine vessels ; and it was
only the presence of a large land force upon the coast
that prevented the victors from dragging away the Syracusan vessels which ran for shelter to Cape Pelorus. Some
days later, the Naxians, aided by some Sicels, with whom
Laches had already established friendly relations, inflicted a bloody defeat on the Messenian land force. But,
despite this double success to the Ionic arms, nothing of
real importance was effected ; and the non-appearance
of the new fleet under Eurymedon and Sophocles let slip
the moment for effective action. Those commanders
were ordered to call at Corcyra on the voyage out, and
there to do what they could to assist the popular party
against a body of oligarchs, the refugees from a violent
revolution of the year 427 B.C., who were now entrenched on
Mount Istone and supported by sixty Peloponnesian war-
ships. Demosthenes, a general who had already served
with marked success on the west coast, also sailed with
the fleet, with full permission to use it, up to its reaching
Corcyra, in any way he might please against the Peloponnesian coast. Acting on these instructions, he took
advantage of head winds to raise a rude fortification at
Pylus, an uninhabited headland of the west coast of
Messenia and one of the horns of the Bay of Pylus, whose
entrance is blocked, as though by a natural mole, by the
long narrow island of Sphacteria. Here he was left
with five ships to support him, and here he was besieged
by the whole force of Sparta both by land and sea.
The latter occupied the island with the pick of their
native infantry ; while their fleet, under Brasidas, hastily

recalled from Corcyra, made repeated but unavailing
attempts to force the Athenian position. But Eurymedon
and Sophocles had already hurried back to the spot, and
the Lacedemonian fleet was driven ashore and with difficulty
secured from capture; the infantry on the island, more
than 420 in number, and 120 of them Spartiatæ, were
blockaded, and the survivors ultimately forced to surrender to a fresh Athenian force under Cleon. It was
not until the twelfth week from the original date of sailing that Eurymedon's squadron was free to pursue its
voyage to Sicily. But whatever hopes the Dorians had
entertained of speedily crushing the Ionic power were
now dashed. Athens, with 292 valuable prisoners in
her hands, and fresh from the glory of having compelled
the invincible Spartans to surrender, was stronger than
ever. The Sicilian Dorians shared in the general depression of their Peloponnesian kinsmen, and became
anxious for peace. Camarina led the way by coming to
terms on his own account with Gela; and shortly afterwards a congress of the Greeks of Sicily was convened
at the latter place to discuss the question of a general
peace, 424 B.C. The leading speaker was Hermocrates,
at the time the chief figure in Syracusan politics, and a
man of pronounced anti-popular opinions. His advice,
however, on this occasion, was patriotic and sound. He
bade the Sicilian Greeks remember that they were
kinsmen, and preserve their own polity without interference from Athens or elsewhere. He pointed out that
Athens was too ambitious to be disinterested in supporting her feeble allies in Sicily, and that she would
not rest content with merely vindicating their liberties.
The congress fell in with his views, and a general peace
was sworn, 424 B.C.

By the pacification of Gela the Athenian commanders
were deprived of all excuse for their further stay in
Sicily, for not only her allies—the Ionic cities—but
Athens herself, was included in the peace. Accordingly,
Eurymedon and his colleagues, with their whole force of
more than fifty ships of war, returned to Athens. The
only result of their presence in Sicily was the temporary

union of all the Hellenes of the west, from a common
distrust of Athenian interference.

On their return to Athens about the beginning of the
summer of 424 B.C., they found themselves impeached
for collusion with the Sicilians. For the previous twelve-
months the fortune of war had been all on the side of
Athens. The landing of Demosthenes at Pylus had been
the first of a series of events which had brought humiliation upon Sparta and triumph to her rivals. The occupation of Cythera threatened the naval stations and
entire sea-board of Laconia—'Better for her had
Cythera been sunk in the sea'—while the seizure of
Minoa and the port of Megara threatened to give the
Athenians command of the Isthmus of Corinth and shut
up the Peloponnesians within their own borders. Everywhere the Athenian fleet commanded the seas. Finally,
and most important of all, 120 Spartan aristocrats and a
still greater number of inferior Spartans had been brought
home at once as prisoners and hostages from Sphacteria
by Cleon. The populace were in no mood to listen to
any tale of failures, even of lack of success. Pythodorus
and Sophocles were banished, Eurymedon escaped with
a fine; and a fresh opportunity for interference in
Sicilian affairs was eagerly awaited.

No sooner had the Athenian fleet retired than the
democracy of Leontini found themselves exposed to the
hostility of their own oligarchic faction, supported as
before by Syracuse. To strengthen their position, they
enrolled a large number of new citizens, and contemplated
a new division of their lands in order to provide allotments
for the new-comers. Such a measure, of course, threatened the estates of the wealthy oligarchs, and the latter,
by a sudden *coup d'état*, expelled the democracy by
force. They then removed their residences to Syracuse,
and from thence farmed their estates at Leontini.
Leontini itself was deserted, and the fugitive democracy
applied once more for Athenian assistance.

Here, then, was the desired opportunity for fresh
interference, but it came too late. At the battle of
Delium (end of 424 B.C.) the Athenians had been severely

repulsed in an aggression against Thebes, while simultaneously Brasidas, after rescuing Megara, was rapidly winning over to the Spartan cause the Athenian dependencies in Chalcidice. With her hands full at home, Athens only ventured to despatch to Sicily two triremes under Phæax, with orders to organize an anti-Syracusan party in the island, with a view to more extensive future action in that quarter (422 B.C.). Before anything material could be effected, the peace of Nicias (421 B.C.) once more diverted her attentions. The Syracusans, having got rid of Leontini, now proceeded to get rid of its few representatives, the oligarchs, who had transferred themselves to Syracuse. Compelled to leave that city, they made an effort to re-establish Leontini in conjunction with a few of the exiled democracy. The attempt failed ; the Leontine territory passed into the hands of Syracuse, and its entire population went into exile, some of them at Athens.

At length, 416 B.C., arrived an embassy from Egesta, claiming the assistance of Athens on the ground of the alliance effected by Laches, 427 B.C. Egesta, an inland town in the western corner of Sicily, was occupied by a people of unknown, but non-Hellenic, origin. Southward its territory proceeded side by side with that of Selinus, and a quarrel in regard to a strip of border-land led to an appeal to arms. Selinus was one of the most wealthy of the Grecian colonies, and, as the last anti-Carthaginian outpost on the western coast, in a high state of military efficiency. Moreover, it was supported by Syracuse. The only hope of the Egestæans lay in foreign aid, and after appealing in vain to Agrigentum and Carthage, they sent an urgent embassy to Athens. The opportunity of chastising Syracuse for this second attack on an ally seemed at once opportune and just. Supported by the Leontine exiles, and by the oratory of Alcibiades, they so far succeeded as to secure the despatch of special envoys to Egesta to investigate the advisability of an armed interference on the part of Athens.

CHAPTER VI.

The Sicilian Expedition.

Life and Character of Alcibiades—Return of the Envoys from Egesta —Efforts of Nicias to defeat their Appeal—The Mutilation of the Hermæ—Suspicion falls on Alcibiades—Cold Reception of the Athenians in Sicily—Discovery of the Fraud at Egesta—Divided Opinions of the Generals—Flight of Alcibiades—Nicias enters the Great Harbour by Stratagem—Battle of the Helorine Way—Events of 414 B.C.—Effect of Gylippus' Arrival and of Alcibiades' Presence at Sparta—Naval Battles—Attitude of the Sicilian Towns—Arrival of Demosthenes—Failure of his Attacks—The Retreat and Surrender of the Entire Army—Fate of the Generals and Prisoners— Character of Nicias—Results of the Expedition—Its Cost.

ALCIBIADES, to whose influence was due the cordial reception of the Egestæan envoys, with its subsequent disastrous results, represented the self-seeking ambition of the young Athenian aristocracy. Descended alike from the famous Alemacoñidæ and the house of Ajax, and a ward of Pericles, he inherited all the oligarch's contempt for equality and democracy. To him politics were the road to personal aggrandisement, and in them he hoped to find the means to gratify that excessive love of display which characterized his whole life. Albeit a pupil of Socrates, he developed every sophistic and unwholesome quality which his teacher condemned, and in him the enemies of Socrates saw the only result of that 'little learning' which 'is a dangerous thing.' They held the teacher responsible for the pupil's failings, and when they forced the former to drink the hemlock, they believed themselves revenged upon the latter for the ruin in which he had involved his country.

At the present time (416 B.C.) Alcibiades was about

thirty-six years of age. For the past five years he had been an active figure in Athenian politics, first on the philo-Spartan side, later, when he found himself little in favour at Sparta, on the side of the extremists of the opposite party. It was mainly through his influence that the Peace of Nicias (421 B.C.) was rendered null ; and by covertly continuing hostilities he gave to Sparta at Mantinea (418 B.C.) the opportunity of recovering the position which she had lost when that peace was made, while at the same time he prevented Athens from re-cruiting, as she might otherwise have done, the resources exhausted by the previous years of war. The battle of Mantinea frustrated his attempts to extend Athenian in-fluence in the Peloponnesus, and for the time being so far diminished his popularity at home that he narrowly escaped ostracism. Excessive display at the Olympic festivals had served in a measure to lessen the ill-feeling against him, but it had gone far to leave him bankrupt. In the appeal of the Egestæans he saw the means of ac-quiring fame, influence, and wealth, and—not least, per-haps—of frustrating the policy of his bitterest foe, Nicias, whose well-behaved Toryism and decided Spartan sym-pathies brought him continually into collision with the Radicalism of Alcibiades.

In the spring of 415 B.C. the envoys returned from Egesta, and reported that the wealth of that town was amply sufficient to defray the cost of the anticipated war. The Leontine exiles seconded their representations with renewed appeals on the score of religion and blood, and Alcibiades fired the ambition of the multitude by repre-senting Sicily as an easy conquest, and the stepping-stone to the complete overthrow of Sparta, when once its trea-sures and its navies were enrolled under the flag of Athens. There were whispers that even Italy and Carthage were not impossible acquisitions.* With such arguments, material and sentimental, on the one side, the assembly refused to listen to the warnings of Nicias on

* The proposed expedition was warmly supported by the mercantile classes, as likely to open up to them a new and wealthy scene of trade. The rich Athenians supported it for the same reason, hoping thus to be secured from the taxation which had oppressed them throughout the Peloponnesian War.

the other. Immediate war was resolved on, and even when the question was put a second time on another day by Nicias, in defiance of constitutional procedure, the former decision was upheld, and Nicias himself was nominated general conjointly with Alcibiades and Lamachus. Nicias made a final effort to defeat the project by demanding an enormous force, whose very magnitude might, he hoped, frighten the populace out of their sanguine enthusiasm. Again the manœuvre failed, and Athens made the double mistake of attempting foreign conquest while she had war at her very gates, and of placing her forces under the divided rule of two bitter enemies.

A few days before the date fixed for the sailing of the armament it was discovered that nearly all the Hermæ* throughout the city had been disfigured during the night. The impiety of the sacrilege—a sacrilege to be atoned for, according to Grecian belief, by nothing short of the chastisement of the entire State—and still more its systematic completeness and secrecy, filled Athens with panic. An outrage so uniform could only have been committed by many hands ; and the Athenians, full of fanciful terrors, pictured to themselves a widespread conspiracy amongst the numerous oligarchical clubs of the city to subvert the government and admit some external enemy. Suspicion ran riot, and Alcibiades was believed to be implicated in the affair. It was, indeed, quite on a par with many of his avowed misdeeds, and his character was such as to lend itself to the suspicion of treasonable designs. This suspicion his political enemies turned to account by forthwith indicting him for impiety. He expressed himself eager to clear himself at once, but on the plea that an immediate trial would delay the expedition, his accusers contrived to send him to Sicily with the charge still hanging over his head, hoping to poison public opinion against him irremediably in his absence.

* The Hermæ were rude-stone pillars, fashioned at the top into the form of a human head, and representing the god Hermes. They stood at the doors of temples and houses, and in most public situations throughout the city.

The evil omen clouded the departure of the armament, which mustered at Corcyra in the middle of the summer,* and thence crossed to Italy, where it took up its station at Rhegium, to await the return of three light vessels which had been sent forward to Egesta to announce the approach of the united force of Athens and her allies. Their reception had not been encouraging. Of all the Italian towns Rhegium alone treated them with even distant friendliness; and even Rhegium, albeit an Ionic colony, refused to commit itself to any active support until the decision of the other States was learnt. The Dorian colony of Tarentum and the town of Locri both refused even anchorage and permission to take in water. Nor was the news from Sicily more encouraging. The report that a gigantic armament was in course of preparation against them long met with no credence at Syracuse, where the democratic leader Athenagoras ridiculed the warnings of the aristocratic leader Hermocrates, whose information was surer, and who laboured to organize a league against the invaders. It was not until the Athenians actually appeared off the Italian coasts that he obtained any credence, and was enabled, at the last moment, to concert measures for defence. Envoys were sent to the Sicel tribes of the interior, to the Dorian States of Greece, and even to Carthage, soliciting help. Of the Sicels many declined to ally themselves with Syracuse. The Greek States mostly accepted the alliance at once, for the magnitude of the armament and the renown of the Athenians for a time cowed all the Greeks of Sicily into union and accord. Even the Chalcidic States, to whose aid the Athenians ostensibly came, mistrusted their champion, and remained passive, declining, indeed, the alliance of Syracuse, but taking no positive steps in the interests of Athens. The Dorian town of Camarina also remained neutral, out of jealousy of the power of Syracuse. In all Sicily only the one semi-Hellenic town of Egesta was in active co-operation with the armament; and with the return of the three despatch-

* For a description of the armament and its departure from Piræus, see Thuc. vi. 31, 32.

boats came a revelation which showed the worthlessness of that alliance. They reported that the supposed wealth of Egesta was a fiction. The Athenian envoys sent in the previous year to inquire into its extent had been duped by the display of plate and treasure which surrounded them in every house wherein they were entertained. But the valuables which they saw were the same in every case, secretly transferred from house to house as occasion required; and the fraud was now discovered when it was too late. Instead of the cordial welcome and ample supplies, or the terrified submission which they had expected, the three generals found every door closed against them.

And now appeared the evils of the divided generalship. Each of the three commanders proposed a different course of action. Nicias, seeing in the indifference or distrust of the Sicilians the justification of his opposition to the expedition, now proposed to get what supplies they could from the Egestæans, to compel the Selinuntines to make peace with Egesta; and, after thus parading the power of Athens and her solicitude for her allies, to return home. Alcibiades argued that it would be foolish and disgraceful to return with so little done. He advocated negotiations with the Sicels to withdraw them from the Syracusan alliance, and the seizure of Messana, the key of the straits. Then, with allies and supplies assured, they could easily proceed against Selinus and Syracuse. Lamachus alone saw the need of striking a decisive blow at once. He urged an immediate advance upon Syracuse, while that town was still unprepared, and the whole of Sicily standing in wholesome dread of the famous fleet now lying off the coast. This, he said, was the surest way of securing allies, and breaking down the Syracusan league. Undoubtedly he was right; but neither Alcibiades nor Nicias supported him, and he was compelled to acquiesce in the plans of Alcibiades, a compromise between his own judgment and that of Nicias.

The fleet, accordingly, moved southwards to Naxos, which welcomed the Athenians as liberators. Catana, the second remaining Ionic town, they took by surprise, and there established a naval camp. The arrival at this juncture of the Salaminia,* to summon home Alcibiades to stand his trial, interrupted the tide of events. Alcibiades professed his willingness to return, and was allowed to use a vessel of his own. At Thurii he took advantage of this privilege to break his parole and make his escape to Sparta. Nicias and Lamachus were thus left in command; and the former, conducting a portion of his fleet along the northern shores of Sicily, captured Hyccara, a small coast town then at war with Egesta. The sale of the prisoners realized a considerable sum; but a subsequent attack on Hyblæa Geleatis miscarried, and Nicias returned to the camp.

Meanwhile, October had come, and the Syracusans began to despise a fleet which, albeit so admirably equipped, had yet effected so little in a stay of more than two months. Passing from fear to confidence, they meditated an attack upon Catana. Nicias, informed of the design by his partisans in Syracuse, sent thither a Catanæan, inviting the Syracusans to surprise Catana on a stated day, and alleging that there was a strong philo-Syracusan party in the town willing to betray it. The opportunity was eagerly seized, and the surprise entrusted to a body of Syracusan foot and horse; but when the latter arrived before the town, they found the Athenians already gone, and the entire force was at once put about, and hurried back in hot haste to Syracuse. They found that Nicias had taken advantage of their absence to convey the entire Athenian force to Syracuse, and to post it securely on the spot called Dascon, a low-lying space between the mouth of the river Anapus and the suburb of Neapolis, at the back of the Great Harbour. The fleet lay beached behind entrenchments to the number of 145 ships of war, of which 100 were the famous triremes of Athens, and the remainder manned by the scarcely less formidable seamen of her allies. The land force mustered 1,500 native Athenian hoplites, 3,600 heavy allied troops, 700 Athenian marines, 500 Argive troops, and 250 Mantineans

* The State despatch-boat used especially for the conveyance of Theories to the sacred festivals at Delos.

and mercenaries, 480 archers, eighty of them Cretans, the most expert in Hellas, 700 Rhodian slingers, 120 Megarian exiles equipped as skirmishers. The grand total, exclusive of the sailors, was 7,850 troops of all arms. Cavalry alone were wanting to counterbalance the ' invincible ' Syracusan horse, now reinforced by a body of the redoubtable cavalry of Gela.

The Syracusan army, returning from Catana, encamped on the western side of the Helorine Way, which crossed the Anapus at a distance of about three-quarters of a mile from its mouth. The bridge had been already cut by Nicias to prevent the advance, upon his flank, of any force from the southern bank. On the following day the Athenian force drew out to battle in two divisions, the first in a line of eight deep, the second posted in hollow square behind as a reserve. On their left was the Anapus with its steep banks; on their right the outlying houses of Dascon, and the Inner Pool ($\mu\tilde{\upsilon}\chi o\varsigma$) of the Great Harbour. The Athenian hoplites occupied the centre of the line, supported on the right by the Argives and Mantineans, and on the left by the auxiliary troops, slingers, and archers. To hold the latter in check, the Syracusans posted their cavalry and light troops on the bank of the river. Their main body was drawn up sixteen deep, with the Helorine Way in their rear. Their generals were Hermocrates and fourteen others. Expected though it was, the battle yet took the Syracusans by surprise, many of them having left their ranks and being even within the city walls when Nicias sounded the charge. Nevertheless they formed as well as they could, and fought with bravery; and when driven, at length, back to the Helorine Way, they maintained their position there, the Athenians not daring to pursue their advantage further, lest by so doing they should expose themselves to a flank attack from the Syracusan horse. The battle was absolutely without result, for on the same day the Syracusans were able to throw across the river a force which garrisoned the high ground about the temple of Zeus Olympius; and on the following day Nicias embarked his whole force, and sailed away to Naxos and

Catana for the winter, feeling himself unable to maintain a position so near the city without an adequate force of cavalry.

For cavalry accordingly, and a fresh supply of money, he despatched a request to Athens, and busied himself during the winter months in collecting siege-material and in extending his influence among the Sicel tribes. His overtures met with but slight success at Camárina, an important position, as it commanded the roads from Syracuse to the allied towns of the southern coasts, Gela and Selinus. His arguments were counteracted by those of Hermocrates, who was present as the envoy of the Syracusans; and the Camarinæans, after listening to both sides, decided to preserve their neutrality.* An embassy which he despatched to Carthage may possibly have prevented the interposition of that power, for it was not unlikely that she should have preferred assisting her rival, Syracuse, to aiding the Athenians in the destruction of the city which at present offered the best bulwark against the rumoured aims of Athens in Africa. From Etruria there had already reached Nicias spontaneous offers of assistance, and he sent thither envoys to ask for a force of cavalry, preferring the same request to the Sicels, of whom many joined him under their prince Archonides.

The Syracusans, on their side, made preparations to resist the impending siege. They garrisoned Megara Hyblæa, which commanded the approach to the city from the north, and constructed a new wall from the shore of the Bay of Thapsus to the Great Harbour, at some distance in advance of the previous wall of Achradina. These new fortifications protected both Achradina and Ortygia. Finally, at the suggestion of Hermocrates, they reduced the number of their generals from fifteen to three, namely, Hermocrates, Heraclides, and Sicanus, and despatched to Corinth and Sparta fresh requests for help, at the same time seeking to distract the operations of the Athenians by inducing the Spartans to renew their aggressions upon Attica.

* A small detachment of twenty horse had assisted the Syracusans in the recent battle.

About March, 414 B.C., Nicias massed his full strength, now augmented by the arrival of 600 horse, at Catana; and suddenly putting out to sea, landed unopposed at Thapsus, and stormed the heights of Epipolæ, which were only occupied by a small garrison of 600 Syracusan hoplites. This elevation, rising gradually from the city walls in a westerly direction, formed a lofty plateau, guarded on the north and south by steep scarps, and commanding the whole city, together with its harbours. It summit was crowned by the fort of Euryalus, at the point where Nicias ascended. Moving downwards, he immediately fortified a position on the slope within a mile of the walls of Syracuse. From this point, known as 'The Circle,' he commenced to carry blockade walls which should reach to the Great Harbour on the south, and to the Bay of Thapsus on the northern side. The Syracusans attempted in vain to prevent the completion of the works. Their cavalry were worsted by the newly-levied horsemen of Nicias, and their endeavours to interrupt the line of the southern blockade wall by throwing out two counter walls from the city, westward towards the Anapus, were successively defeated. The first wall was stormed and taken by the Athenians with ease. The storming of the second wall brought on a general engagement which cost the life of Lamachus, though not until he had secured the victory for his side. The Syracusans, however, compelled Nicias to burn all his siege engines and material, and only drew off on seeing the Athenian fleet a second time sail into the Great Harbour.

The Syracusans began to despair. They vented their displeasure upon their generals, whom they dismissed from office, appointing three others in their place. The change brought no relief. Supplies failed, and surrender began to be openly discussed. Nicias, confident of speedy success, relaxed his efforts, and even when the news reached him that a Peloponnesian squadron was on its way to the relief of the city, he took no measures to prevent its approach. The Syracusan envoys, on arriving at Sparta, had found their warmest advocate in Alcibiades. Not only did he alarm his hearers with exaggerated reports of Athenian ambition, and urge them to send assistance to their kinsmen in Sicily, but he bade the Lacedæmonians carry the war into Attica and establish a fortified post at Decelea before the very gates of Athens. It was resolved to send help to Syracuse, and Gylippus was ordered to take the command and sail without delay; but only four triremes were provided for him, and these were so slow in appearing that it was June before he could arrive at Leucas. There he awaited the Corinthian contingent of twelve vessels under Gongylus. Tired of delay, he eventually pushed across to Italy without the Corinthian flotilla, and as he had no hope of running the Athenian blockade with his few vessels, he passed along the north coast of Sicily as far as Himera. Here he learnt that the wall of blockade was not, as he had supposed, completed, but that there still remained a narrow passage on the northern side of 'The Circle' between the wall and the outer sea. Rapidly collecting a handful of troops from Gela, Selinus, and some of the Sicel tribes, he marched overland, crossed Epipolæ before the eyes of the Athenian garrison, and entered Syracuse about the beginning of August. Gongylus had through the negligence of the Athenian fleet sailed into the docks of Ortygia but a few days before, just in time to prevent the surrender of the city. .

The presence of a veritable Spartiate amongst them gave new courage to the Syracusans. Without a moment's hesitation Gylippus assumed the offensive. Leading out the Syracusan army as if for battle before the walls, he sent off a body of men who passed along the northern cliff of Epipolæ and captured the Athenian outposts on that side. Having thus cleared the way, he commenced the construction of a new counter-wall which should run from the north-west corner of Achradina through the still open gap in the blockade wall, and so right along the back of Epipolæ to Euryalus.

Nicias began too late to see the folly of his remissness. He felt that he had met his match on land, and proceeded to do what he could for the effective employment of his fleet. He seized the promontory of Plemmyrium, which formed the southern arm of the land surrounding the Great Harbour, and there he built a fortified camp. At the same time he allowed the construction of the counter-wall to proceed unmolested until it had all but intersected his own lines of blockade. To prevent this he at length gave battle on the eastern slope of Epipolæ. The first encounter resulted in the retreat of the Syracusans, but did not leave Nicias able to carry their works ; and when the struggle was renewed on the ensuing day, his entire force was defeated and the counter-wall pushed far up the slope towards Euryalus. The blockade was raised on the landward side, and within a few -hours Erasinides sailed into port with twelve triremes from Corinth, Ambracia, and Leucas.

So completely was the position of the belligerents reversed, that Nicias was now, as he himself confessed, rather the besieged than the besieger. The necessity of guarding the blockade wall, useless though it was, prevented his employing his full land force ; while the Syracusans, flushed with success, began to molest even his fleet, and were rapidly getting together a flotilla almost as numerous as his own. Ill-success brought with it disaffection, and the desertion of slaves and mercenaries rapidly increased. The unhealthy position of Plemmyrium generated sickness in the camp, and Nicias himself, now sole commander, had for some time been prostrated by illness. The garrison at the Olympieum continually harassed his foraging parties, while Gylippus was actively busied in raising fresh troops from the native and Hellenic towns. Finally there was no small probability that the Italian cities, upon whom depended the supplies of the Athenians, would declare for Syracuse. Ashamed to retreat, Nicias sent home an urgent despatch detailing his difficulties, and praying for additional reinforcements of men, ships, and money, and for his own recall. The only result was the continuation of Nicias in command with Menander and Euthydemus as his colleagues, and the immediate mission of Eurymedon with ten ships to carry to him a supply of money, with the assurance of fresh and large succours in the early spring.

Meanwhile other envoys from Syracuse had visited Corinth and Sparta, again urging the need of striking a decisive blow at the power of Athens. Slow to believe as they proverbially were, the Spartans were at length convinced that their opportunity was come, and at the very moment when Demosthenes sailed from the Piræus with the promised reinforcements, the Peloponnesian army was entrenched at Decelea, and the vengeance of Alcibiades began to make itself felt. None the less was Demosthenes suffered to sail away carrying with him sixty Athenian triremes and 1,200 citizen hoplites, besides other vessels and troops of the allies. Simultaneously a fleet of thirty ships of war was despatched to ravage the coasts of Peloponnesus. There seemed no limit to the resources of Athens.

While Demosthenes was pressing forward to Sicily, the Syracusans had resolved to attack their enemies even on the water. Suddenly sailing out of their docks with eighty vessels, they were met by sixty Athenian triremes hurriedly and imperfectly manned. A stubborn fight at length left the latter victorious, but on returning to their moorings they found their camp at Plemmyrium in the hands of the enemy, who had surprised and captured the position under cover of the diversion created by the sea-fight. The hoplites escaped on board the transports, but almost the whole of the stores and the military chest became the prize of the Syracusans, who now occupied the harbour-mouth on both sides. The Athenians were thus cooped up at Dascon, cut off alike by sea and land. Immediately after this event the whole of the Sicilian cities, with the exception of Naxos, Catana, and Agrigentum, declared for Syracuse, and despatched a strong force to the scene of action. Nicias had, however, still sufficient influence to induce the Sicels to attack and disperse this force when on its way to Syracuse.

Towards the end of June the Syracusan fleet, after weeks of desultory skirmishing, provoked another general engagement. Having, as usual, made a feint of attack, they retired to their position at Ortygia, and the Athenians, believing the action ended for the day, disembarked and prepared to take food. Suddenly their enemies sailed out a second time in full line, and bore down direct upon Dascon. They were unable to break the mole which protected the Athenian naval station; but in the battle which ensued they gained a decisive victory. They were disappointed of its fruits; for within twenty-four hours Demosthenes entered the Great Harbour with seventy-three vessels and 5,000 heavy infantry, besides a large number of mercenaries and light troops.

The new general, now acting as a colleague of Nicias, saw that something decisive must be done at once. He immediately assumed the offensive, and endeavoured to recover Epipolæ, the possession of which must determine the success or failure of the siege. Finding the attempt to storm it futile, he determined to surprise it by night; but, like many another night attack, this also miscarried, and the new troops suffered heavily. His whole force had moved after dark up the valley of the Anapus, and, turning to the right, they ascended the ridge at Euryalus, and carried the western extremity of the Syracusan defences. Flushed with success, the van rushed forward without awaiting the arrival of the remainder of the column, and as they hurried in disorder down the slope they were met by a small phalanx of Bœotians in the Syracusan service. In a few moments their victory was turned into a rout, and the entire Athenian force driven in utter confusion to their camp.

Demosthenes was now convinced of the futility and danger of any further stay, and would at once have returned home. But Nicias was still ashamed to do so, and it was only on the entry of yet another force of Sicilian auxiliaries into Syracuse that he was induced to consent. Secret orders were given that all should be in readiness for departure when, on the night of August 27, occurred an eclipse of the moon. Nicias had always been excessively superstitious. He saw in this phenomenon an evil omen, and declined to stir until thrice nine days had elapsed. Before that date the Syracusans had learnt his intended departure and determined to prevent it. Their fleet, now seventy-six strong, engaged the eighty-six vessels of the Athenians in a third battle. Already disheartened and demoralized by ill-success, inactivity, and sickness, the Athenians were further hampered by the lack of room for their evolutions. Their whole line was defeated; their right wing, under Eurymedon, was destroyed in its entirety and the crews captured; while the remainder of the fleet was only saved by the success of the land force in a pitched battle, in which their Etruscan allies did signal service. The Syracusans followed up their victory by blocking up the entrance to the harbour, so as to render impossible any attempt to escape by sea.

In breaking this mole lay the only hope of escape for the Athenians; and a few days later Nicias, though only with infinite difficulty, induced his men to embark for a fourth and final effort. As before, seventy-six Syracusan vessels joined issue with Nicias' fleet, which was augmented by every means possible to a total of 110. For hours the fight lasted, and was ended by the absolute triumph of Syracuse, and fifty triremes were either destroyed or fell into the victors' hands.*

No persuasion could bring the defeated men again to risk a sea-fight. Nothing remained but to force a way, in the face of the ubiquitous Syracusan cavalry, to some friendly town; and on the morning of the second day, about September 15, the camp was broken up. Forty thousand men of all arms marched out and pushed up the valley of the Anapus in the direction of the friendly Sicel tribes, with the intention of wheeling to the right from the interior, and so reaching Naxos or Catana.

But the Syracusans, who had already succeeded in delaying the departure of the Athenians, by a stratagem until their own troops were recruited and sobered after the recent victory, now harassed the foe unceasingly. Food and water ran short, and on the second day the retreating army found itself checked by a Syracusan force posted above the road at Acræ. For two days they endeavoured to force the pass, while wounds, starvation, and despair thinned their ranks by thousands; and in

---

* The description of this fight in Thuc. vii. 70, 71, is one of the most powerful pieces of descriptive writing in the Greek authors.

the ensuing night, leaving their camp-fires burning as usual, they silently wheeled about and directed their march to the coast, hurrying along the Helorine Way towards Camarina and the southern parts of the island. The first division, under Nicias, contrived to effect the passage of a stream in the face of a Syracusan picket, and proceeded unmolested; but the second, with Demosthenes, fell into disorder, made but slow progress, and, after a day of continuous fighting, were entrapped on the banks of the stream and forced to surrender. Two days later Nicias himself capitulated on the banks of the Asinarus. Of the 40,000 who left Dascon six days before, less than 10,000 remained alive. Both generals were taken prisoners.

Nicias had surrendered to Gylippus on the assurance of the latter's protection. As the prime mover in the peace called by his name, and active in ameliorating the lot of the Spartans captured at Sphacteria, he had deserved and won the gratitude of the Lacedæmonians. Demosthenes, on the other hand, was, as the author of their humiliation at Pylos, no less their most hated foe. Aware of this, he had endeavoured, but in vain, to kill himself when his troops capitulated. Both he and Nicias were condemned to death to satisfy the animosity of Syracusans, Corinthians, or Spartans, as the case might be; and the utmost that Gylippus could do, despite his claims for indulgence, in his efforts on their behalf, was to provide them with the means of committing suicide. The mass of the prisoners were reserved for further horrors. Shut up in the stone-quarries of Epipolæ, half starved, ill-clothed, with no shelter from sun or frost, and sickening from the stench of their comrades' unburied corpses, they died in crowds within their prison, a spectacle for the wives and children of the conquerors. But very few escaped to return to their homes.

From the case of Nicias the Athenians learnt how disastrous may be the best efforts of those who 'have greatness thrust upon them.' Pre-eminent in his native city for his 'almost superstitious piety,' for his cautious policy, and for a sort of traditional respectability and munificence, he was utterly unfit for command in a position where everything depended upon bold and unhesitating action. Caution and procrastination were qualities rooted in his very nature. He was known to be set against the expedition; he was the private and public opponent of one of his colleagues; he was a confirmed invalid. Yet he was forced into undertaking what he felt to be a reckless, improvident, and unprovoked aggression. Good-fortune relieved him of the colleague whom of all men he most hated, and left him with Lamachus for his coadjutor; and had Lamachus lived, the expedition might yet have succeeded. But Lamachus fell at the very moment when foresight and discipline and boldness were most essential; and, left to himself, Nicias suffered his army to 'grow old along with its sick general.' When Demosthenes, a more able and vigorous commander than even Lamachus, arrived, the mischief was done. (A fatal superstition and a false pride prevented the withdrawal of the armament while it was yet possible, and completed the ruin which remissness had begun.) And yet the patient long-suffering of the sick man merited something more than contempt, and it is a kindly criticism that, 'had he not been commander, he would have been of all men most worthy to command.'

So ended the first and last attempt of the Athenians to subjugate Sicily. Henceforward the history of Sicily remains, as before, isolated from that of the rest of the Hellenic world, and becomes more than ever the history of Syracuse. That this city should now by common consent take the first place in the island was the due reward of victory—a victory indisputably her own in so far as expenditure of blood and money was concerned. But in reality the victory was that of Sparta, whose representative, Gylippus, had saved a falling cause, and by his mere presence had enabled the still opulent city to use its resources with effect. And the consequences of the victory were far-reaching. It ultimately brought upon Syracuse the full tide of Carthaginian jealousy; it crushed the last hopes of the non-Dorians in Sicily; it paved the way for Dionysius' conquests in Magna

Græcia ; it at once added a new and active foe to those already swarming upon Athens ; and by destroying her prestige, even more than her power, it brought Nemesis upon that city. From first to last Athens must have lost 80,000 men. Three generals fell, while a fourth became the avenging spirit of Athens. The enormous cost of the war may be estimated from the fact that the pay of the Athenian triremes alone could not have been less than 1,500 talents (£375,000), apart from that of the transports, the troops, and the initial cost of the two armaments. But Syracuse had withstood, had destroyed all, albeit she had no confederacy of allies whose accumulated tributes could be turned to the rescue of the city.

CHAPTER VII.

Dionysius I

Enthusiasm at Syracuse—Active Operations against Athens—Hermocrates in the Ægean—His Banishment—Diocles — Egesta appeals
to the Carthaginians—Hannibal—Sack of Selinus and Himera—
Attempts of Hermocrates to re-enter Syracuse—First Appearance
of Dionysius—Siege of Agrigentum—Its Desertion and Sack—Disgrace of Daphnæus—Dionysius elected a General—His Intrigues—
He becomes Sole General—He obtains a Bodyguard, and becomes
Tyrant —Fails to relieve Gela—Suppresses a Rising in Syracuse,
and makes Peace with Carthage—Fortifies Ortygia and disarms the
Populace—Popularity of his Resolve to make War on Carthage.

THE triumph of Syracuse at the close of 413 B.C. left her
full of hatred for the power which had brought upon her
so much suffering. Few things are more surprising in
ancient history than the elasticity with which a Greek
State recovered from blows apparently crushing. Syracuse—and indeed Athens also—proved no exception to
the rule. In spite of the waste, both of citizens and of
treasure, entailed by two years of war, despite the desire
for peace which that war must not unnaturally have
aroused, the Syracusans, having once tasted revenge,
determined to follow up their success to the end. To
have destroyed the flower of the Athenians' forces, together with two of their most esteemed generals, was not
sufficient—the very vestiges of their empire were to be
swept away. Party spirit was forgotten in the enthusiasm of the moment, or rather all parties were merged
in the wave of liberal democracy which, commencing
before the year 415 B.C., had been the chief instrument
in the defence of the city, and now gained additional

6

impetus from its proven stability. At the head of the aggressive movement was Hermocrates—his reputation augmented by the zeal with which he had ⁻supported Gylippus ; while the latter doubtless lost no opportunity of urging the city which owed its safety to himself and to Sparta, in turn to assist Sparta in her crusade against Athens, the 'enslaver of Greece.' Scarcely waiting to re-organize their relations with their Sicilian allies and the few still hostile towns like Catana, the Syracusans despatched, in the spring of 412 B.C., a squadron of twenty triremes, under Hermocrates, to join the great fleet which the Peloponnesians had in that year sent out under the supreme *navarch*, Astyochus. Selinus sent two other vessels, and Thurii, which had lately passed over to the anti-Athenian side, furnished a squadron of ten under Dorieus. After her enormous losses in Sicily, none of her friends or enemies imagined that Athens could hold out for another year.

The proceedings of Hermocrates and the Sicilian contingents in the Ægean belong more properly to the history of Central Greece than to that of Sicily. For four years the combined Peloponnesian fleets carried on a desultory maritime war about the Hellespont and the coast of Asia Minor, but the proverbial tardiness of Sparta, coupled with the double-dealing of Alcibiades and Tissaphernes, neutralized their greatest efforts. The former had incurred the personal enmity of the Spartan king Agis, and the distrust of the Peloponnesians at large, and was now, in 411 B.C., a refugee with Tissaphernes, the Persian satrap or governor of the southern parts of Asia Minor, intriguing for his recall to Athens. Tissaphernes, while pretending to favour the Spartans, was in reality playing off the two belligerent powers each against the other for his own advantage, and paralysing the efficacy of the Lacedæmonian fleet by bribes. Hermocrates and Dorieus, themselves incorruptible, accused their confederates of venality. Astyochus was superseded by Mindarus ; but the new *navarch*, though active, was unsuccessful. He was defeated in three successive engagements, at Cynossema (411 B.C.), Abydos (410 B.C.), and at Cyzicus (409 B.C.). The last defeat cost him his life and annihilated his whole fleet. The Sicilian contingents shared in the disaster, not a vessel escaping, while their crews were left destitute on the eastern coast of the Hellespont. At the close of 409 B.C. the Syracusans at home, already disappointed of their confident expectations of vengeance, heard with dismay the gist of the famous despatch in which the surviving Spartan commander described his position : ' We are ruined. Mindarus is dead —the men are starving. We know not what to do.' In a fit of most unreasonable exasperation they decreed on the spot the banishment of Hermocrates and his fellow-officers, despatching others to take under their command the survivors of the defeated squadron.

Two causes combined to bring the Syracusans into this spiteful temper—the revival of party animosities and the renewal of hostilities with Carthage.

The unanimity of parties which had prevailed after the overthrow of the Athenian armament does not seem to have lasted long. Its early action was marked by the appointment of a Board of Ten, headed by Diocles, a Syracusan of wide influence throughout Sicily, to revise the laws and constitution of the State. The appointment of *Nomothetæ*, or law-givers, is a sufficiently common occurrence in earlier Grecian history, but after the year 500 B.C. becomes anomalous, and the commission of Diocles is a proof of the lamentable condition to which years of revolution and reaction had reduced the State. Diocles seems to have justified his selection by the rigour of his legislation, particularly as regarded the adminis-tration of justice, although we have no particulars of his reforms.* Until the conquest of Sicily by the Romans the laws of Diocles remained the basis of all later Syra-cusan codes ; and were even adopted by other States, such as Selinus. But there seems to have been no sufficient security against unconstitutional reaction, for within five years of their promulgation they were overthrown by the

* With the exception of the substitution of the lot for voting in the appoint-ment of magistrates—a peculiarly democratic innovation. Still it seems that the lots must have been worked in the interest of the oligarchs.

tyrant Dionysius, who posed as a demagogue. This fact points to a sudden revival of the old quarrel between the aristocracy and the masses, and the banishment of Hermocrates, himself an oligarch, could have been carried only by the popular party as a spiteful assertion of its powers for the moment. One additional proof of internal dissension may perhaps be found in the fact that Syracuse was unable during a war of three years to reduce the towns of Naxos and Catana—a fact scarcely conceivable unless her energies were crippled by faction at home.

The exasperation arising from the ill-success of their arms alike in the Ægean and Sicily was now accentuated by the danger of attack from Carthage. Since the year 480 B.C., when Hamilcar and his entire army were destroyed at the battle of Himera, the Carthaginians had remained passive spectators of Sicilian affairs, contenting themselves with their three trading stations on the west coast. The original cause—dread of Gelo of Syracuse —had given place to fear of Hiero, his successor, and that in turn to apprehension of the superb navy of Athens. They had welcomed with delight the overthrow of the bulk of that navy at Syracuse—an overthrow which seemed to have left even the conquerors in the extremity of weakness. Everything promised success when, in 410 B.C., Egesta invited the protection of Carthage against Selinus.

This town, the westernmost and most Carthaginian of all the Hellenic cities of Sicily, had profited by the troubles of Syracuse to secure a wide influence in the island, leagued with Agrigentum and Gela. The vaunted and futile effort of Athens to champion Egesta had on the other hand made that town the object of universal antipathy, so that, when about the year 411 B.C. a dispute arose concerning some borderland, Selinus was able not only to settle the quarrel in her own way, but further to attack the recognised territories of Egesta. The Egestæans, without Sicilian or Greek allies, were compelled to throw themselves on the mercy of Carthage at the moment when any interference by that State seemed likely to be most successful. It happened, too, that the chief suffete at the time was Hannibal, grandson of the general who fell at Himera, who had been compelled to spend many years of his life at Selinus as an exile in expiation for his grandfather's ill-success. He had recently returned to Carthage, where, with unbounded influence in the State, he retained a hatred of all that was Grecian and a Hannibalic thirst to revenge the defeat of his ancestor. He had no difficulty in persuading Carthage to take up his cause; and by the close of 410 B.C. it was well known that he would invade Western Sicily with a Carthaginian force, typical in numbers and ferocity. Hannibal was, moreover, a diplomatist as well as a soldier. He despatched envoys to Selinus to remonstrate with that State for her aggressions against Egesta, and to suggest that the quarrel should be submitted to the arbitration of Syracuse. The Selinuntines, in the flush of success, declined; while the Syracusans, thus rejected as arbitrators, at once declared themselves neutral, exactly as Hannibal had wished and expected.

In the summer of 409 B.C. the Carthaginian army landed at Motye, and advanced at once upon Selinus. That city was taken completely by surprise. The peace party, headed by Empedion, had been silenced, and every overture refused; but no defensive measures seem to have been taken to support so offensive an attitude, beyond appealing to Agrigentum and Gela for reinforcements. Those reinforcements never arrived, for after ten days of continuous assault, Selinus was in the hands of the Carthaginians, it walls were razed, its temples desecrated, and all its inhabitants, save some 3,000 who escaped to Agrigentum, were either slain or made prisoners.

The fall of Selinus roused the Sicilians to action. Syracuse threw off her neutrality; and 5,000 men, with contingents from various other towns, commanded by Diocles, were at once thrown into Himera, whither the Carthaginian army moved direct from Selinus. Again the storming engines of Hannibal were brought up, and a ceaseless attack was maintained. For a few days the besieged held out, and then in a sudden sally drove back the advanced posts of the enemy with heavy loss. But the appearance of the reserves under Hannibal completely changed the face of events. He drove the Greeks once more into the town with the loss of 3,000 men, while at the same time came the news that his fleet was putting out from Motye to sail round to Syracuse, now nearly stripped of its military forces. Diocles at once hurried his whole force homewards, and ordered the Syracusan squadron which occupied the harbour of Himera to retreat likewise, carrying with them as many of the useless population as possible. On the next day Himera was carried and razed. Of the prisoners, Hannibal selected 3,000, and sacrificed them on the scene of his grandfather's defeat to the spirit of that general. He then founded a new town, Thermæ, in place of Himera, disbanded his whole force, and sailed home to Carthage.

At about the same time (end of 409 B.C.) Hermocrates landed at Messana. After the disastrous battle of Cyzicus, he had busied himself in providing for his destitute crews; and his personal influence with Pharnabazus, satrap of the northern parts of Asia Minor, had enabled him to obtain a large grant of money and permission to build vessels from the forests of Mount Ida. When the new commanders arrived from Syracuse with the despatch announcing the condemnation of Hermocrates, the latter was able to hand over to them a well-equipped squadron, who, however, murmured loudly against the injustice shown to their late admiral. Hermocrates silenced their murmurs, adjuring them to use nothing but peaceable means to secure his restoration; and betook himself again to Pharnabazus, who furnished him with fresh funds and ships with which he at once sailed for Sicily, resolved to effect his return by force. He found, however, that his own party was still in the minority, for the oligarchs, and particularly Diocles, were at the moment in bad odour, as having caused by their remissness the destruction of Selinus. An attempt to surprise Syracuse was frustrated, and Hermocrates drew off to the ruined site of Selinus, where he established himself as the leader of refugees from that town and from Himera, and harried the Carthaginian reservation with impunity, there being now no army to oppose him. Thus proclaiming himself the avenger of the destroyed Greek towns, he gathered fresh adherents, while the influence of the rival party of Diocles sank proportionately. Accordingly, in 408 B.C., Hermocrates again moved upon Syracuse. On this occasion he trusted to a stratagem to secure his entry into the town, for he carried with him the bones of those Syracusans who had fallen before Himera, and professed to be desirous only of placing them in the sepulchres of their fathers. Any appeal to Greek sympathy on the score of reverence to the dead was politic and powerful; and the determination of Hermocrates to make himself despot must have been notorious indeed to counteract such an appeal. Party feeling ran high between the two factions, and ended, not in the recall of Hermocrates, but in the banishment of Diocles also. The bones of the victims of Himera were buried with ceremony, but Hermocrates was forced to content himself with earning an additional reputation for piety, and to retire once more to Selinus. A few months later, summoned by his partisans within Syracuse, he surprised Achradina, but was immediately slain by the forces of the opposite faction (407 B.C.).* Most of his followers were slain, the remainder banished, and many who escaped were declared by their friends to have fallen in the battle that they might thus avoid the sentence of exile.

Amongst this number was Dionysius, at once one of the keenest partisans of the democratic faction, and the most assiduous in exalting the prowess of the slain Hermocrates against Carthage at the expense of Diocles and the oligarchic party.† Of low birth, he had practised as a public scribe, and may possibly have been already of

* The dates of these various attempts of Hermocrates to effect his return are quite conjectural. Grote gives those which are here adopted. The difficulty of the subject is increased by there being at the time two persons named Hermocrates in Syracuse, the second of whom was the father of Dionysius.

† It would seem that the Hermocratean oligarchs, disappointed of their object, now coalesced with the democrats, hoping by these means to overthrow a rival clique of anti-Hermocratean oligarchs.

some reputation as an author, for in later life he wrote a number of odes and tragedies. Having been wounded in the final attempt of Hermocrates to enter Syracuse, he remained in the city in concealment, and shortly afterwards appeared publicly as the leader of the democratic party, though we are not told how he continued to avoid the punishment which fell upon most of the defeated Hermocrateans. Probably the expectation of the presence of the Carthaginians in Sicily in 406 B.C. diverted from party politics the attention of the oligarchic faction, who remained satisfied with their recent success.

It seems that Hannibal, having avenged the defeat of Himera and successfully supported Egesta, was desirous of no further aggressions. But the daring of Hermocrates in raiding the lands of Motye and Panormus, coupled with the confidence inspired by the easy capture of Selinus and Himera, roused the Carthaginians to fresh efforts, and in 406 B.C. a force of 150,000 men landed at Motye under the command of Hannibal and Himilco. The former had at first declined service on the plea of age, but was finally persuaded to sail on the appointment of Himilco as his colleague. The intentions of Carthage had been no secret in Sicily. The various towns had been actively engaged in preparing for resistance, more particularly Agrigentum, which now stood as the western fortress of Hellenism, and was consequently the primary object of attack. The town was built on a cluster of hills rising as high as 1,100 feet from sea-level, at the southern margin of the most fertile plain of fertile Sicily. On one side alone was there an approach to the walls which encircled the town—a town which could not have numbered less than a quarter of a million of inhabitants. The slight records of its political history prove that it must have escaped in great measure from the troubles which continually exercised its rival Syracuse; while the purposed humiliation of the neighbouring town of Gela by Gelo had left Agrigentum without a peer on the southern shore of Sicily. Her wealth, her temples, her fortifications,* the luxuriance of her crops of grapes and olives, were famed throughout Sicily ; while her name was proclaimed repeatedly before all Greece as the home of victors at the Olympic games. Three hundred of her citizens could furnish racing cars drawn by teams of white horses to welcome home one of their number, the victor at the games of 408 B.C. The walls of Selinus had been old and weak ; but those of Agrigentum seemed impregnable when the Carthaginian army drew its lines about the city immediately after landing. Dexippus, a Spartan, had been summoned from Gela to conduct the defence, and the siege had already lasted for some time when the Sicilian contingents from Syracuse, Gela, Camarina, and other places, arrived under the command of Daphnæus, the successor of Diocles as head of the oligarchic party at Syracuse. Routing a body of horse which endeavoured to bar his progress, Daphnæus entered the city in safety. But unfortunately for himself he had withheld his men from following up their victory, wisely foreseeing that their disorder would put them at a disadvantage when Hannibal's reserves attacked them. For the same reason Dexippus had held his garrison in check ; and now both generals were loudly accused of collusion with the enemy. They escaped for the moment, but four of their Agrigentine colleagues were at once indicted and stoned to death unheard, the sole command being vested in Daphnæus.

The Greek forces were now large enough to set at defiance any attempt to storm the town, and the Carthaginian generals settled down to reduce it by blockade. For many months little progress was made, while a violent sickness, breaking out in their crowded lines, carried off numbers of them, including Hannibal himself, and filled the rest with superstitious terrors. They had destroyed the magnificent tombs which filled the plain on the south side of the town, using the materials in their siege works. This impiety was now recoiling on them,

* Arduus inde Acragas ostentat maxuma longe Mœnia, magnanimum quondam generator equorum. — Æneid. iii. 703. The Greek name Acragas expresses the position of the town on cliffs.

they thought, and as an expiation the customary human sacrifices were offered. The siege dragged on into the eighth month, and was at one time almost abandoned through the mutiny of the mercenary troops, who clamoured for pay ; while the whole army suffered from the difficulty of getting provisions. A squadron of Carthaginian vessels contrived to surprise a large convoy of supplies off Agrigentum, and so relieved Himilco's army, while scarcity began to be felt in the town. The mercenaries of Dexippus mutinied and marched away. The fidelity of the remaining troops was doubtful ; and at length the order was given to evacuate the town by night. The majority of the garrison and inhabitants thus escaped ; but some who preferred to share the fate of their homes were cut down or burnt in the ruins of the town when it was occupied by Himilco in the morning.

The return of Daphnæus and his colleagues to Syracuse was the signal for an outburst of popular fury. It gave to the democratic party a new and powerful handle against the discredited oligarchs. When the generals appeared before the assembly to explain their conduct, they were met with nothing but insult and clamour, until finally Dionysius, now the recognised champion of the combined democrats and Hermocrateans, openly accused them of treachery and bade the populace stone them there and then, as the Agrigentines had done with their own treacherous citizens. Rebuked by the presiding officers, Dionysius only became more reckless and violent, and in the end the generals were dismissed in disgrace, and a new board, including Dionysius, was elected in their place.

Who were the colleagues of this arch-demagogue we do not know, except that amongst them were Philistus, the historian, and Hipparinus, a ruined aristocrat who threw in his fortunes with those of the rising demagogue. It may be regarded as certain that all the members of the board were chosen from the ranks of the popular party which was at the moment synonymous with the party of Hermocrates and Dionysius. But this unanimity of political views did not improve matters. Dionysius began to obstruct his colleagues in every possible way, and by incessant accusations of treachery to poison against them the minds of the Syracusans. The fate of Agrigentum, and the ever-present menace of the advance of Himilco upon Syracuse, had thrown the city into a condition of panic and alarm in which the populace was ready to suspect everyone, while Hipparinus and his fellow-generals doubtless played into the hands of Dionysius. The latter now declared that, within the city, there were none to be trusted, and that the only true patriots were the exiled partisans of that Hermocrates who had so well proved his loyalty by avenging the ruin of Selinus. On their recall, he said, depended the safety of the State. He carried his point; and from all parts of Sicily there flocked back to Syracuse men who owed their late exile to the oligarchy, their restoration to Dionysius—men eager to do his bidding to any extent, so that it gave them revenge upon their enemies.

Meanwhile the Carthaginian general had remained encamped at Agrigentum collecting the plunder of that city, and had held his army together during the winter instead of dismissing it in the usual way. His next object of attack was Gela; and the Geloans, aware of their danger, urged the Syracusans to assist them in defending their city. The Lacedæmonian Dexippus had already brought into the town a detachment of his mercenaries, and the Syracusan generals now marched out to his support. At Gela had appeared the same panic and mistrust as at Syracuse, and the oligarchic party were regarded by the populace with detestation and mistrust. Again Dionysius stood forth as the champion of democracy. He provoked the Geloans to rise, massacre the oligarchs, and confiscate their belongings. The proceeds of the outrage he applied to paying his troops so lavishly as to secure their loyalty. Instead, however, of marching against Himilco, he suddenly withdrew and returned to Syracuse, taking with him also the troops of Dexippus, and so leaving Gela absolutely defenceless at the very moment when the approach of Himilco was most imminent. Arrived in Syracuse, he styled himself the 'liberator' of the Geloan democracy, and stood higher than ever in popularity. In the burst of enthusiasm which greeted him, he secured the deposition of his colleagues in a body, and his own appointment as sole general, with unlimited powers.

The plea for such a course was solely the need of decisive action against the Carthaginians; and had Dionysius been the patriot he professed himself, he would at once have moved westward to prevent the investment of Gela. But patriotism did not trouble the new dictator. He had obtained his advancement by the free and spontaneous act of the democracy; he determined to secure it before the inevitable reaction could occur. Tyranny had but one protection, its bodyguard; and to obtain this also by popular vote Dionysius had resort to another piece of double-dealing. He ordered the whole force of the city to march out to Leontini, which had remained, since the Sicilian expedition, a dependency of Syracuse, occupied on sufferance by a number of exiles and refugees. There was no excuse for an armed demonstration in that quarter, least of all by a general whose appointment was intended to check the ever-increasing danger of Carthaginian attack. In consequence, such of the citizens as suspected the attitude of Dionysius failed to appear in arms in obedience to his summons, and he marched out accompanied only by his own adherents. Encamping at Leontini for the night, he suddenly caused an alarm to be raised, and declaring that an attempt had been made upon his life, he induced his army to allot to him a bodyguard of 600 men.* He at once proceeded to select twice that number of the most needy and reckless desperadoes obtainable, whom, with a standing army of mercenaries collected from all quarters, he secured to his service by the gift of magnificent armour and by the promise of high pay. He then marched without molestation through Syracuse to Ortygia, the citadel, where he permanently established himself, after procuring, by popular vote, the execution of Daphnæus and other leading oligarchs, and the

* The regular word for a soldier of the bodyguard in Greek is δορυφόρος, a spearman, from the lance carried by the bodyguard of the Great King.

dismissal of Dexippus. At the same time (beginning of 405 B.C.) he married the daughter of Hermocrates. It now remained to secure himself from the attack of Himilco, who was already besieging Gela. Marching overland, Dionysius appeared before the Carthaginian lines with 30,000 men, while a fleet of fifty sail supported him by sea. The siege now assumed the same character as had been the case at Agrigentum, and for three weeks went on a desultory warfare without decisive results to either side. At the end of that period Dionysius made arrangements for a general attack. His fleet, assaulting the Carthaginian lines on the seaward side, where they were least securely defended, actually carried the works ; and had the land forces come up, as arranged, to attack the position at other points, victory would probably have been with the Greeks. But there is every reason to believe that such a result was purposely avoided by Dionysius. To set the Sicilian Greeks free from Carthage would be to leave them at liberty to act with Syracuse against himself, while he had no scruples about using the aid of Carthage to confirm his own power. The land attack was made too late, while the particular regiment which formed the despot's strength was never brought into action at all, so retaining its courage and numbers unimpaired. Himilco drove off the attack of the fleet, and the Geloans now learnt that their pretended defender had resolved to evacuate the town, albeit he had suffered little loss, and the position remained as tenable as ever. Like Himera and Agrigentum, Gela was abandoned in the darkness ; and Dionysius afforded a further proof of treachery by compelling the inhabitants of Camarina to join in his flight and abandon their city, thus surrendering that position also, the last outpost of Syracuse towards the south.

An act of such palpable cowardice or treason, which-ever it was, aroused to revolt the Syracusan soldiery, already regretting the part which they had played in the aggrandisement of Dionysius. The cavalry, the finest troops in Sicily, mutinied in a body ; and finding the usurper's person too securely guarded to admit of their reaching him, galloped off to Syracuse, announced the treason and flight of Dionysius, occupied his stronghold of Ortygia, and plundered the property of the despot and his adherents. They declared the city once more free, and gave themselves up to their feelings of delight and satisfaction. But Dionysius had already divined their purpose. He pushed on towards the city at full speed, and on arriving at the gates about midnight he found them virtually unguarded. To force an entry and fight his way to Ortygia was a small task in the confusion and disorder of his enemies. Those of the horsemen who could effect their escape retreated with their partisans to Ætna. The refugees from Gela and Camarina established themselves at Leontini.

Syracuse apparently lay at the mercy of Himilco whenever he chose to attack it, but at this juncture he made peace with Dionysius. It appears that a pestilence, similar to that which had attacked his army before Agrigentum, had recurred and carried off upwards of half of his troops—a fact which sets the retreat of Dionysius from Gela in a still worse light as an act of collusion. It would, moreover, serve Himilco, on his return to Carthage, as an excuse for having stayed his hand when all Sicily seemed at his mercy; and doubtless it would appear an easier thing to leave Dionysius pledged as a vassal of Carthage to the maintenance of peace in the island, than to attempt the permanent occupation of Sicily. Accordingly, peace was signed on the following conditions. The Carthaginians retained all their earlier dependencies and possessions in the west of the island, together with Selinus, Himera, and Agrigentum. Gela and Camarina were restored to their inhabitants as tributaries of Carthage, on condition that those towns should remain unfortified. Leontini, Messana, and the Sicel communities were to remain autonomous. On the other hand, the Carthaginian government recognised, and undertook to support, the despotism of Dionysius over Syracuse.

Himilco thus secured a sort of over-lordship in Syracuse, while in Gela and Camarina he possessed frontier positions little less hostile to the despot than to Carthage. The independence of Leontini and of the Sicel tribes completed the chain of control to the west and north, depending as they did upon Carthaginian influence for their own autonomy. The fortress of Agrigentum, the key of the southern coast, passed, with its extensive trade, into the hands of Carthage, whose reservation was thus extended beyond the Halycus to the line connecting that town with Himera.

Thus left to himself, the despot proceeded to render Ortygia an impregnable position. He surrounded with enormously strong walls not only the whole of the small peninsula, but also the Lesser Harbour (*Laccius*), in such a way as to admit of but one vessel sailing in or out at a time, while a fleet of sixty sail could lie secure within its basin. Hither he collected his bodyguard and mercenaries in specially constructed barracks. At a later date he fortified also the city proper, enclosing the larger and eastward portion, Achradina, within one continuous wall, to which the walls of Tyche on the north-west, and of Neapolis on the south-west, formed appendages or loops, each complete in itself. Between Ortygia and Achradina lay a narrow strip of low ground, averaging half a mile in width, which remained vacant, and was used as a necropolis. The descent of Epipolæ was also fortified, though not all at once. For the present, Dionysius contented himself with carrying a wall along the northern and more accessible scarp from Tyche to Euryalus, thus barring the approach of any enemy from the side of Leontini and the Bay of Thapsus. The marshes of the Anapus and the more difficult character of the southern slope seemed, for the present, an adequate defence on that side.

The enormous cost of these works was met by heavy exactions from the citizens, whose murmurs broke out into open mutiny in 403 B.C. At that time the whole citizen army was encamped before Erbessus, a Sicel town, which had sided with Carthage in the recent war. They killed their deputy-commander, Dorieus, and, marching upon Syracuse, occupied Epipolæ, where they were joined by auxiliaries from Rhegium and Messana, and by the exiled horsemen from Ætna. They even sent envoys to Corinth to ask for assistance ; but that State, their metropolis, was in no position to spare an armed force, and could do no more than send one Nicoteles to support the insurgents by his advice. The latter were now strong enough to occupy the necropolis and lay siege to Ortygia, while a Rhegine and Messenian fleet blockaded it by sea, and cut off all supplies. Starved out, Dionysius was on the point of surrender, when the over-confidence of his foes saved him. Feeling their success assured, the besiegers relaxed their vigilance, and the despot was able to negotiate with a body of Campanian mercenaries, whose sudden arrival raised the siege. Dionysius used his victory with moderation. He allowed the remnant of the insurgents to withdraw to Ætna, and took no sanguinary measures against the citizens at large. He seized, however, an early opportunity, during the ensuing harvest-time, to search the houses of the townsmen then absent in the fields, and to appropriate all their arms.· He built also additional vessels and fortifications ; but his power was above all strengthened by the active countenance of Sparta. That State, fresh from her victory over Athens, was now busied in overthrowing democracy everywhere, and substituting for it oligarchies and *harmosts*, whose government was little else than despotism under another name. With this access of moral support in addition to his extensive material resources, Dionysius successively attacked and reduced Catana, Naxos, and Leontini ; and when the Italiot Greeks of Locri and Rhegium, aided by Messana, menaced him with attack, he avoided a conflict, and was able by skilful diplomacy to put himself on good terms with all three States. He even asked· a wife from Rhegium, and though the request was refused with contumely, he was more successful in a similar application to the Locrians. He married Doris, daughter of a distinguished citizen of that place, taking at the same time a second Syracusan wife,* Aristomache, daughter of Hipparinus.

---

* His first wife, daughter of Hermocrates, had been put to death by the insurgent horsemen, 405 B.C.

From his marriage with Doris dates the beginning of the long alliance between Locri and the Dionysian dynasty— an alliance fatal to the welfare and liberties of much of Magna Græcia.

His mild policy towards Rhegium and its allies was due to a desire to conciliate all parties, and so be free to carry out his designs against Carthage. The idea of driving the Carthaginians out of Sicily was as popular now as ever ; and when the despot declared himself about to champion the cause of Hellenism against the Barbarians, desisting at the same time from the violence and cruelties which had marked his first tenure of power, he found ready support throughout the majority of the Greek towns in the island. For three years he busied himself with ceaseless preparations for war. His arsenals were stocked with many thousand stand of arms of the finest workmanship. New siege engines, notably catapults, were invented, and vast trains of artillery got together. His fleet was augmented to 300 sail, and amongst them were vessels larger than any as yet seen in Grecian warfare, ships of four and even of five banks of oars.*

* *I.e.*, Quadriremes and Quinqueremes. The trireme, or ordinary vessel of three banks, carried on each side three tiers of thirty oars each, and about twenty marines or fighting seamen, a total of 200 men.

CHAPTER VIII.

Dionysius I.—(*Continued.*)

The War with Carthage—Excellence of the Opportunity—Siege of
Motye—Himilco relieves Egesta—Sacks Messana—Naval Victory of
Mago—Siege of Syracuse—Relations of Dionysius with Sparta—The
Plague—Flight of Himilco—Increase of Dionysius' Power—Wars in
Italy—Condition of Magna Græcia—The Native Tribes—Sack of
Rhegium—Plunder of the Temple of Agylla—Actions of Dionysius
in the Adriatic, and elsewhere—His Theory at Olympia—Oration of
Lysias—Fresh War with Carthage—Assists the Spartans against
Thebes, etc.—His Tragic Victory, and Death—His Character,
and Patronage of Literature.

IT was in the beginning of 397 B.C. that Dionysius, now
fully prepared for war, commenced his aggressions by
surrendering the lives and properties of all Carthaginian
residents in Syracuse or the dependent cities to the
mercy of the Sicilians. Their mercantile proclivities
prompted many of that people to reside in the Sicilian
coast towns, so that they offered an easy and lucrative
plunder to their enemies. A herald was then despatched
to Carthage, bidding that power withdraw from all the
great cities of Sicily on pain of war. The moment was
well chosen. The same pestilence which had thinned
the armies of Himilco before Agrigentum and Gela,
eight years before, had crossed to Africa, and had for
three years or more been devastating the territories of
Carthage. So paralyzed were the Government that no
measures seem to have been taken to counteract the
declared aims of Dionysius, for he was allowed to subjugate
the Sicels and the Greek towns at his pleasure, despite
the special clauses in the recent treaty guaranteeing their

independence, as well as to manufacture arms without hindrance. Even the garrisons of the newly-conquered towns of the south coast had not been augmented beyond their ordinary peace footing ; so that when Dionysius appeared in succession before the gates of Camarina, Gela, Agrigentum, and Selinus, with a land force of 80,000 foot and 3,000 horse supported by a fleet of nearly 500 sail, these towns at once welcomed him as a deliverer. The garrisons were massacred and sold as slaves, and in the spring of the same year (397 B.C.), Dionysius laid siege to the oldest and most important of the native Carthaginian settlements, the town of Motye. The intense hatred of the Hellenes for the Carthaginians is well illustrated by their thus deliberately transferring themselves to the power of a notorious despot like Dionysius.

The siege of Motye was no slight matter. The Carthaginian element was almost unmixed in the western corner of Sicily, and the scattered fortresses of the Elymi— Egesta and Eryx—were more Carthaginian than Greek. Entella was occupied by a body of mercenary troops, recently in the service of Carthage, and not inclined to transfer their support to Dionysius ; while the actual coast-line was entirely commanded by the great fortresses of Motye, Panormus and Solus. Nevertheless, the Syracusan force was sufficiently large to lay siege to Motye while detaching various divisions for action against the other positions of the interior. Of the latter, Eryx fell into the hands of Dionysius ; but the remainder, closing their gates, defied him, though unable to prevent his troops from ravaging the whole country at will. The town of Motye itself was built on an islet in the small bay on the northern side of the Promontory of Lilybæum, and was connected by a bridge with the coast. On the approach of the enemy the bridge had been destroyed, and Dionysius was compelled to construct a mole from shore to shore—a distance of 1,200 yards— before he could bring his engines within reach of the walls. But the mole was at length completed and the siege commenced in earnest. The Carthaginians, alarmed, as they well might be, at the rapid progress of their enemies, were only able to despatch Himilco with a fleet to act as he best could in defence of their countrymen. That general, not venturing to face the magnificent fleet of Syracuse in the open sea, endeavoured first to raise the siege by a descent upon Syracuse itself; but, though the squadron sailed into the harbour there and destroyed some merchant vessels, the recently erected fortifications prevented their doing any further damage, and they returned without creating the intended diversion. Himilco now attempted to surprise Dionysius' fleet while it lay beached in the Bay of Motye, and it was only rescued from destruction by the vigorous action of the despot. He caused eighty of his vessels to be transported bodily across the Promontory of Lilybæum to the sea on the other side, and Himilco, thus threatened with a flank attack, was compelled to retire to Carthage. Soon afterwards the town fell by a nocturnal surprise, and Dionysius, leaving his Admiral Leptines in command, with orders to continue the operations against Entella, Egesta, and other towns, retired to winter at Syracuse.

In the following year, 396 B.C., he rejoined Leptines, and personally conducted the siege of Egesta, which still defied his efforts. While thus engaged he received news that Himilco had effected a landing at Cape Pelorus with a force of 100,000 men and more than 2,000 ships, including transports. The landing had been effected by night, and Himilco had taken successful precautions to prevent Dionysius learning the destination of the force which he knew to be gathering. An attack by Leptines failed to prevent his advance, and moving upon Motye, the Carthaginian army reoccupied that place without any serious resistance. Dionysius, thus robbed in a moment of the toil of so many months, and finding himself short of supplies, retreated to Syracuse without hazarding an engagement.*

Having thus relieved the besieged towns, Himilco determined to take vengeance on the Greeks for the sack of Motye. The Hellenic towns of the south coast, so recently pillaged by his troops, offered little hope of

* Lilybæum was founded now, to take the place of Motye as chief fortress and mart of Carthage in Sicily.

booty, nor were there any noteworthy cities on the north coast. He resolved to transfer his forces at once to the eastern coast and to attack Messana, the key of the straits, a town whose position, in the most remote corner of the island, had protected it as yet from the assaults of Carthage. Accordingly he marched along the northern coast, receiving as he went the allegiance of the Sicel tribes, who hated Dionysius as the destroyer of that independence which Carthage had by treaty secured for them. Feigning a land attack, he induced the full force of Messana to quit the town and advance to meet him; whereupon his fleet sailed unhindered into the harbour and took the place at once. The plunder, if less rich than that of Agrigentum, was sufficient to repay the trouble of the attack; the town was rased to the ground and left a wilderness. The whole Carthaginian force now moved southward upon Syracuse, skirting the coast, and so acting in conjunction with the fleet under Mago.

It is difficult to understand what could have kept the Syracusan army inactive during this time, for some months must have now elapsed since the retreat from Egesta. That retreat had been viewed as an act of cowardice by the army, and the old murmurs were again heard accusing the despot of collusion with the enemy. Such a charge was on this occasion ridiculous; but certainly little had been effected to justify the immense preparations and the great force—the largest ever under Greek command—which had been collected in the previous year. So widely had the discontent spread that when Dionysius at length marched northward to meet Himilco he had with him but 30,000 men. Off Catana his fleet gave battle to the flotilla under Mago. The battle was stubbornly contested, but ended in the complete defeat of the Syracusans, with the loss of 100 vessels and 20,000 men. Dionysius at once retreated without venturing to engage their land force, and shut himself up in Syracuse, sending urgent requests for assistance to Sparta and Corinth. The whole Carthaginian fleet at once sailed into the great harbour; Himilco, with his army, fortified a camp at the Olympieum and outposts at Plemmyrium and

Dascon; and twenty years after the Athenian expedition the Syracusans saw themselves once more threatened with ruin by an enemy occupying the same ground as Nicias.

This second retreat of Dionysius lent new energy to the discontent. Mutiny spread among his mercenaries, and was with difficulty checked. He now exerted himself to recover some of his lost prestige, and personally conducted flying squadrons to protect the convoys which still reached the Syracusan harbour, despite the vigilance of Mago. At the same time he declined to hazard a general engagement either by land or sea. He was absent on such an expedition, when a citizen named Theodorus gave expression to the general discontent. A chance engagement in the harbour, brought on by the endeavour to seize a Carthaginian transport, had left the Syracusans triumphant. Theodorus thereupon bade them for the future cease to trust Dionysius, whose generalship brought nothing but disgrace, and whose despotism was misery. Let them disown him, and fight for themselves; for the recent fight had shown that they were more favoured of heaven than were the arms of the murderer and temple-plunderer who was their despot. Dionysius reappeared while the assembly was still undecided, and with him came Pharacidas, the leader of the succours from Sparta. The question depended on his decision, for to offend Sparta was to provoke the greatest power in the Greek world—a power fresh from the overthrow of her enemies, and triumphant throughout Greece. But it was no part of Spartan policy to favour democracy. She was already seeking the alliance of Persia and of Alexander, Tyrant of Pheræ in Thessaly. She now allied herself with an equally infamous enemy of Hellenic liberty, and through the mouth of Pharacidas declared for Dionysius and tyranny. The Syracusans, deprived of their one hope of support, were cowed into acquiescence, and Dionysius was once more free to continue his despotism.

This stroke of good fortune was followed by another which had still more important results. The plague, which had so often decimated the armaments of Carthage, again broke out in the camp of Himilco with appalling virulence. His men died by thousands, while the Syracusans were untouched. The marsh fevers which had wasted the troops of Nicias were as nothing to the pestilence which now converted the whole camp of the Carthaginians into a mortuary. The wall which Dionysius had constructed on the northern slope of Epipolæ had nullified all attempts at blockade ,by leaving open the road into Syracuse on the northern side, and Himilco seems never to have attempted to carry Euryalus, the key to the whole position. Pestilence completed what stupidity had begun. Dionysius could watch the host of his enemies melting away, and could choose his own time for striking. Repeating the manœuvre of Gylippus, he marched round the enemy's line and took them in the flank, while his fleet attacked and burned the whole Carthaginian flotilla and the camp at Dascon. Only dread of contagion prevented his occupying Himilco's lines at once. He drew off and awaited the approaching end. It soon arrived. Himilco endeavoured to negotiate for the safe retreat of his whole force. On this being refused, he made a secret treaty by which his own escape and that of the other native Carthaginians in his army was assured, and putting to sea by night, sailed away to Africa. His deserted army, left without a general, fled in all directions, pursued by the Syracusans. The Hiberians alone were spared, being taken into the pay of the despot (autumn, 395 B.C.). Himilco, publicly declaring his defeat to be the just reward of his sacrilege in destroying the tombs on the Helorine Way before Syracuse, starved himself to death. But the prostration of Carthage was completed by the revolt of her Libyan subjects, who, to the number of 120,000 men, occupied Tunis, and shut up the Carthaginians within their walls. It was only at the last extremity that the Queen of Africa was able to crush the revolt by means of an opportune quarrel among the insurgents. She was long incapacitated from fresh interference with the power of Dionysius, though her Admiral Mago maintained a vigilant attitude at the western corner of Sicily, and there by his conciliatory conduct won over many of the neighbouring towns to the Carthaginian side.

The first care of Dionysius was to re-establish Messana, which he peopled with adherents of his own, intending it as a *point d'appui* in his meditated attacks upon Southern Italy. At the same time he reconstituted Leontini as an independent town, giving it to some 10,000 mercenaries whose mutinous clamours for pay had put him in a dangerous position. Then marching westward, he recovered all the ascendancy which Himilco had wrested from him in the two preceding years, seizing, in addition, Enna, Cephalœdium, and Solus in the extreme west, and making alliances with the various Sicel chiefs.

In the year 393 B.C. he laid siege to Tauromenium, which, the strongest position in north-east Sicily, had been captured by Himilco in 396 B.C., and by him handed over to a body of Sicels. These new colonists offered so successful a resistance that Dionysius was unable to effect their reduction despite all his efforts, and only narrowly escaped with his life in a fruitless night attack. His ill-success led to the defection of Agrigentum, which seems to have remained dependent on Syracuse since its recovery from the Carthaginians in 397 B.C. It now declared itself autonomous, and expelled the party of Dionysius, while its example found imitators among many of the recently conquered Sicels. Even Mago was encouraged to take the field anew. He ravaged the newly-organised territories of Messana, but was compelled to retire with loss on the appearance of the despot.

In the following spring Dionysius undertook his first expedition against the Italiot Greeks. He had never forgiven the insulting reply of the Rhegines on his demanding a wife from their number. The only fit wife for him, they had answered, was the daughter of the common hangman. He resolved to take a terrible vengeance on Rhegium, and suddenly appeared before the walls with a powerful force. It was only the courage of Heloris—once a personal friend of Dionysius, but now an exile—which saved the town; and the Syracusan forces were drawn off before anything further could be done in order to meet Mago, who was again advancing. The armies met at Agyrium, the capital of the Sicel prince Agyris, and Dionysius was able to prevent the capture of the town. Mutiny in his own army prevented his further progress, and he availed himself of Mago's offers to conclude a peace by which the Sicels of Tauromenium were surrendered to him. Attacking that fortress again in the following year, he at length reduced it, and repeopled it, like Leontini and Messana, with mercenaries of his own. He was thus firmly in command of the narrow strait which divided him from the scene of his next conquest.

The cities of Magna Græcia were not unaware of the danger which menaced them from Syracuse, but unhappily they were harassed at the same moment by an even nearer danger. The Samnites, the hardiest mountain race of central Italy, descending from their fastnesses in the Apennines, had spread over Campania, ousting the Etruscans of Capua, the Greeks of Cumæ and Neapolis, and forcing the Lucanians to move southward also, in search of new lands.

The origin of these Lucanians is doubtful, as is also their relationship to the Bruttians, the prior occupants of the 'toe' of Italy. Probably both were branches of the same Samnite stock; but the Bruttians were now becoming the serfs of their Lucanian invaders, whose power had already overthrown one or two Greek cities on the coast, such as Laus and Pæstum, and now threatened the independence of the others.

To meet these aggressions there had been formed a defensive league of all the Greek cities, from Thurii to Rhegium, Locri alone standing aloof. That state was already connected with Dionysius by his marriage with Doris; it now became his active ally to satisfy its private jealousy of the neighbouring city of Rhegium. Its secession was sufficient to paralyze the action of the Italian league, by furnishing to Dionysius a secure basis of operation at the moment when fresh attacks of the Lucanians threatened the independence of Thurii. He was now in alliance with the Lucanians, and his landing at Locri and instant march upon Rhegium was the signal for a simultaneous descent of the Lucanians on Thurii (390 B.C.). The latter enterprise was so successfully repulsed that the Thurians, grown over-confident, followed up their foes into the heart of the mountains, and were there entrapped, losing 10,000 men out of a force of 14,000. The 4,000 who escaped did so by swimming to the Syracusan fleet, which was coasting off the scene of their defeat, under the impression that it was 'the allied squadron of Crotona. Leptines, the Syracusan admiral, despite their hostility, suffered them all to depart safely at a small ransom; for which act of humanity he was dismissed by Dionysius, who handed over the command to his brother Thearides. He was at the moment smarting under the complete failure of his attempt on Rhegium, where a storm had destroyed the second division of his fleet, while he himself escaped to Messana with the greatest difficulty.

In the following year he redoubled his efforts, aiming in this campaign at the reduction of the cities generally. With 20,000 men and a large fleet he laid siege to Caulonia, on the northern borders of the Locrian territory. Heloris, now elected commander-general of the entire Italiot forces of 25,000 men, marched to the relief of the place, but was himself surprised and slain with his leading division, while the remainder of his army was defeated, surrounded, and at length forced to capitulate, to the number of 10,000 men, under pressure of thirst. Dionysius, by a stroke of humane policy—strangely at variance with his usual conduct—set them all free, thus disarming much of the opposition to his aggression. Then, a third time attacking Rhegium, he forced that town, now isolated, to surrender on promise of clemency—a promise which he seemed to fulfil in exacting only the surrender of the entire Rhegine fleet and 100 hostages. Soon afterwards he took both Caulonia and Hipponium, a town on the western coast, north of Rhegium, and handed over the territory of both to Locri. In the following year, determined still to wreak full vengeance on Rhegium, he picked a new quarrel with that town, now virtually disarmed, and laid siege to it for the fourth and last time. It made a desperate resistance, but fell at length; and when Dionysius marched through its gates, there remained alive but 6,000 inhabitants, whom he sold into slavery. Their commander, Phyton, he put to death with a cruelty borrowed from the Carthaginians, and the town he utterly destroyed. He then returned to Syracuse, where, as signs of his wide-felt power, he found waiting him envoys from those Gauls who in 390 B.C. sacked Rome, and who now begged his alliance (387 B.C.). A few months later he extended his Italian power by the capture of Croton, the strongest position in the South Italian peninsula; and prompted, perhaps, by his Gaulish allies, made a piratical descent upon Pyrgi, the port of the ancient Etruscan town of Cære, where he plundered the immense treasures of the temple of Leucothea. His excuse was the suppression of Etruscan piracy; but the real reason was doubtless the wish to recruit his exhausted treasury, in which he amply succeeded.

It was in that year, the ninety-ninth Olympiad, Dionysius despatched a magnificent Theory* to Olympia, to compete in the chariot-races and dramatic contests, and to parade before the eyes of assembled Greece the wealth and power of his dominion. At that festival was present the famous orator Lysias, once a citizen of Thurii, but now domiciled at Athens. Amid the general decay of patriotism, Lysias retained some of that feeling which had animated the Greeks a century before; and he now saw with disgust the purple magnificence of the Syracusan commissioners, the representatives of a tyranny which had lately overthrown the free Greek state of Rhegium, and reduced many others to dependence. He addressed the assembled crowd in a violent harangue, in which he spoke of Dionysius as the firebrand that was scorching the Western, just as Artaxerxes was consuming the Eastern part of Hellas. The multitude took up his text with such ardour that they attacked the tents of the Syracusan Theory, tore them to pieces, and assaulted the

* Θεωρία, a sacred embassy, representing its particular State at any religious event.

persons of the sacred commissioners themselves. At the same time a poem, which Dionysius caused to be recited at the games, was received with hissing and hooting. So infuriated was Dionysius on hearing of these events—the symbol of the universal hatred of Greece—that he is said for a time to have gone out of his mind.

The matter seems to have prompted him to actions which might render his position less invidious, and he now prepared for a fresh war with Carthage. After erecting an additional wall along the southern slope of Epipolæ, and including the suburb of Neapolis within the city walls, he advanced, in 383 B.C., to meet Mago. At a battle near Cabala, the position of which is unknown, he defeated and slew that commander, with the loss of 10,000 men, suffering the remainder to depart on condition that the Carthaginians would at once evacuate Sicily. The son of Mago, succeeding to his father's position, made excuses for some days' delay, until he had restored the confidence of his army. Then, attacking the Greek army at Cronium when unprepared for any renewal of hostilities, he utterly destroyed it. Night alone saved the remnant. 14,000 dead were left on the field. Dionysius was forced to make peace by ceding Selinus and much of the territory of Agrigentum, thus constituting the river Halycus the boundary between his own dominions and those of Carthage, and by paying so heavy an indemnity as to make Syracuse for the time the tributary of Carthage (382 B.C.). Some Carthaginian efforts in Italy were less successful, and he was able there to maintain his ascendancy; and he even contemplated the construction of a wall across the peninsula of Bruttium from sea to sea, to protect the Locrian territories from incursions on the northern side.

For the remaining years of his life we have only incidental information of the actions of Dionysius. We know that, as an ally of Sparta, he sent a squadron of ten vessels to act with her against Athens and Bœotia, 373 B.C.—a squadron which was captured in its entirety by Iphicrates —while he also supplied some small bodies of mercenaries to the Spartan army. He seems to have been husbanding his strength in order to revenge his recent humiliation by Carthage, and in 368 B.C. he took the field once more with 33,000 horse and foot, and 300 ships of war. His efforts were at first successful, and he mastered Eryx, Entella, and Selinus. He next laid siege to Lilybæum— the new fortress constructed by the Carthaginians after the sack of Motye—but, being surprised here by the unexpected appearance of a Carthaginian fleet of 200 sail which he believed to have been destroyed in dock by fire, he lost 130 ships which were lying in the harbour of Eryx to blockade Lilybæum by sea, and withdrew to Syracuse. The Carthaginians contented themselves with his repulse and with the recovery of the towns which he had lately occupied.

In the early months of 367 B.C. the news reached Syracuse that the despot poet had been at last successful in his efforts to win the prize of Tragedy, though only at the Lenæa, a second-rate Attic festival. On this occasion only had he obtained the first place, and in the excitement of his delight he indulged too freely in a banquet celebrating his triumph. His excesses brought on a fever of which he shortly died, leaving behind him in the tragedy of his own life the example *par excellence* to Grecian moralists of the misery of the tyrant's position. His reign of thirty-eight years is said to have cost the lives of 10,000 victims to his personal cruelty, exclusive of the thousands who fell in his endless wars; and in the height of his power he went in such dread of assassination that he would suffer no barber to dress his hair, but singed it with his own hands, and searched the persons of even his wives and brothers for the dagger which he believed them to conceal. Yet his courage and boldness are indisputable, and the great Scipio, who in later days conquered Carthage, pronounced him one of the two Greeks who excelled in military ability. The other was Agathocles, his successor fifty years later as despot of Syracuse. Nevertheless, when he died he had done little to beat back the enemy of Sicily, and at his death the Sicilian domain of Carthage was inferior to that which she had held on his accession only by the strip of territory which lies between the Halycus and the Himera. With all his oppressions he seems to have been decidedly a man of culture, and the success of his literary activity proves him to have had no mean taste for refined pursuits. In this he resembled Hiero, as also in his liberal patronage of men of letters; and his court presented the singular spectacle of a group of men each distinguished for his excellence in philosophy or literature, yet all supporting a *régime* repugnant alike to their convictions as thinkers and as Greeks with a loyalty which endured when Dionysius himself was gone. His chief ministers were Philistus, the historian, whose attachment to the despot dynasty even exile could not shake, and Dion, an ardent disciple of Plato. The great philosopher himself visited Syracuse in 387 B.C., and if he found his theories of government distasteful to the despot, such a result probably surprised no one but himself and his fellow-enthusiasts.* The failure of his endeavours to regenerate Dionysius did not damp the ardour of his disciples, and Dion still retained his influence, checking for the present the violence of his master, and looking forward in the future to greater influence with that master's successor.

* He was seized by Dionysius, and sold into slavery.

CHAPTER IX.

Dionysius the Younger.

THE double marriage of Dionysius the Elder resulted in a large family—three sons born of the Locrian Doris, two other sons, Hipparinus and Nysæus, and as many daughters, born of Aristomache, daughter of Hipparinus the Syracusan. The eldest, both of the sons of Doris and of the whole family, was Dionysius the Younger, now about twenty-five years of age; but the great influence of Aristomache, herself a native-born Syracusan, threatened to set aside the son of the Locrian queen and substitute for him her own son Hipparinus. Dion, the most trusted of the ministers of the late despot, one of the wealthiest men in Syracuse, and undoubtedly the person of most influence both within and without the city, was brother of Aristomache, and therefore brother-in-law to the dead Dionysius. He was married to Arete, one of the daughters of Aristomache, while the other was wife

Genealogy of the Dionysian Dynasty.

405—343 B.C.

Doris = Dionysius I. = Aristomache
of Locri.   d. 367 B.C.   of Syracuse, murdered by Hicetas.

Hipparinus

(a son)

Dionysius II.
b. 392(?) ; deposed 343 B.C. ;
married Sophrosyne.

(a son)

Hipparinus,
despot, 353 B.C.
(assassinated).

Nysaeus,
succeeded Hipparinus ; deposed 346 B.C.

Dion, b. 408, d. 353 B.C.

Sophrosyne,
married Dionysius II. ; murdered by the
Locrians, 346 B.C.

Arete,
married (a) Thearides,
brother of
Dionysius I. ;
(b) Dion ;
murdered by
Hicetas.

Apollocrates,
surrendered
Ortygia,
355 B.C.

(a daughter)

(a daughter)

(a son)

Murdered by the Locrians,
346 B.C.

of the younger Dionysius, to whom Dion was therefore related by marriage as at once brother-in-law and uncle. On the other hand, he was by blood the uncle of Aristomache's sons; and it seemed not unlikely that he should lend his influence to advance Hipparinus. His philosophy may have led him to disappoint the partisans of Aristomache. He at once recognised the succession of Dionysius the Younger, and by sound advice and sincere support acquired with the son the same authoritative position which he had possessed with the father. Foreseeing the probability that Carthage would now push more vigorously the war which had been languishing for some months, he pointed out the best measures for ensuring the security of the State, putting at the service of Dionysius both his person as an envoy to Carthage, and his property for the purpose of equipping an adequate fleet. Money would seem to have had particular value in the eyes of the new despot, whose exchequer was either exhausted by the long maintenance of his father's standing army and fleet, or by his own indulgences, or was possibly sealed by his niggardliness.* Dion's vigorous action prevented any *coup* on the part of the Carthaginians, and the war apparently came to an end about 366 B.C. None of its details are known, but it seems to have been carried on in part about the Lucanian coasts, which had been threatened even during the life of the elder Dionysius.†

But the chief interest of the early years of the reign of Dionysius the Younger lies in their relation to the political philosophy of the times. The essence of Greek life was political activity. The passion for isonomy,‡ or political equality, was innate in every Hellene, and its successful assertion had led to the overthrow of the older monarchic and despotic governments, either actually or virtually,

* The forces of Syracuse were at the moment on a war footing, said to have amounted to 400 vessels and 100,000 men. That money difficulties occurred a few years later (360 B.C.), we know from the revolt of the mercenaries, although the interval seems to have been one of peace. See p. 118.

† See p. 108.

‡ 'Ισονομία (*lit.*, equality of laws), and 'Ισηγορία (*lit.*, equality of speech), are with Herodotus synonyms for democracy in its most complete form; *i.e.*, as it appeared in Athens 510 to 410 B.C. Herod. V., 78.

throughout Greece. No less national was the tendency to philosophic speculations; and the union of. these two motives was the characteristic of the Pythagorean School of Philosophy, which from its original home at Crotona extended itself over most of the cities of Magna Græcia. At Crotona the Pythagoreans had formed, as early as 500 B.C., a kind of secret society which became of such importance as to incur the suspicion of oligarchical designs;* and the populace had driven them out, murdering many of their number. Similar outbreaks had occurred in other cities against similar clubs; and, taught the dangers of dealing with politics in any but the popular spirit, the remnant of the brotherhood for the future avoided any public parade of their opinions. Much of the thought of Western Hellas was transferred about the same time to the Eleatic School,† which concerned itself more with speculations in ethics and natural philosophy. There still remained, however, many distinguished thinkers, such as Archytas of Tarentum, who nursed their theories with constancy, and waited for the time when they might realize them.

The same distrust of philosophy which had resulted so disastrously to the Pythagoreans extended, though in a less degree, to all schools of thought. The philosopher was called eccentric and useless, even if no graver charges were brought against him.‡ Unpractical he certainly was, and finding himself unable to be a politician in his own fashion he withdrew entirely from the political world — a procedure quite antithetic to the natural tendency of the Hellenic mind. But the troubles which beset Greece in the later years of the fifth century B.C. — the aimless chaos of parties, the failure of all patriotism, whether national or civic, and the growing yoke of external domination—tended to spread amongst all men

* This was largely due to the mysticism, ascetic seclusion, and freemasonry of the Pythagoreans. What they cannot understand is always viewed with suspicion by the vulgar.

† So called from Elea (Velia), on the Gulf of Posidonia, in western Lucania, where it was founded by Parmenides, and maintained by his successor, Zeno.

‡ Socrates was put to death at Athens, 401 B.C., on the ground that he corrupted the young, and neglected the Gods. The Athenians really revenged upon him the misdeeds of his pupil, Alcibiades, the black sheep of his flock.

disgust for practical politics, and the desire to find in philosophy some panacea for the ills of time.

Succeeding to the schools of Pythagoras and Parmenides in the West, that of Socrates' pupil, Plato, was now established at Athens as the centre of thought and science. Eminently practical in the hands of Socrates, it had already become speculative and mystical in the hands of Plato, even previous to the year 387 B.C., when that philosopher first visited Italy and Sicily. In the course of this visit he had made the acquaintance of many of the leading representatives of the older Western schools, and the symbolism of Pythagoras and of the Eleatics had so far blended with the true Platonic doctrines that the Western philosophers, attracted also by the brilliant genius and winning manner of Plato, now looked up to him as the leader of all philosophies alike. According to the Platonic theory, true happiness was attainable only in the State wherein the rulers were philosophers. Power and knowledge must be combined; and the mind that had been trained up to value virtue and truth could alone administer the affairs of a people for their welfare. In brief, the Platonic theory claimed to have found the key to the long-studied problem, How to combine philosophical with political activity. Such a theory had attractions for all men ; for while it promised to free the philosophers from the disfavour and disabilities under which they laboured, it promised also to stop the decay of political life, to revive patriotism, and to remove by the gentle means of reason and argument the despotisms which already enthralled half Hellas, which threatened soon to absorb the other half, and which had so often proved themselves too strong to be overthrown by force.

To all these theories Dion, then merely a young aristocrat of the ordinary stamp, and the first adviser of a despot to boot, had given a ready ear when Plato had first visited Syracuse ; and so well had he laid them to heart that, despite the disgrace into which Plato fell, the pupil became one of his most ardent disciples. He laid aside the habits of Sicilian luxury and indulgence, which had attained a proverbial notoriety in Greece, and became an ascetic. With the Elder Dionysius he could do nothing, and he was too prudent to risk his whole fortune in the attempt. He reserved his efforts until the accession of Dionysius the Younger put the control of the greatest power in Hellas into the hands of one whom Plato himself describes as ' able to think, and willing to learn,' and who, at the same time, was bound to him by the ties of blood, and of a long-established respect. Constituted at once chief political adviser of the new despot, he lost no time in making himself also Dionysius' tutor ; and he impressed upon him so successfully the beauties of philosophy, that he was able within a few months to send to Plato the most pressing invitations to revisit Syracuse—invitations backed up warmly by Dionysius himself, as well as by the united voice of the philosophers of Italy and Sicily. Now was the time to realize the Platonic ideal. A magnificent city, the capital of a wealthy empire, was at the disposal of one young and tractable mind, itself at the disposal of the ' God of Philosophers.' If Plato would but come and reason, as he only knew how to reason in the cause of philosophy, Syracuse might become the seat of that union of power and knowledge which was to save Hellas, and regenerate the world. The appeal was irresistible. Though sixty years of age, and enjoying at Athens all that the widest influence and respect could give him, Plato could not bring himself to fail his disciples at the crisis of their hopes ; and in the year 367 B.C., he once more landed in Syracuse.

Had he but proceeded at once to take advantage of the momentary enthusiasm of Dionysius, all might have been well. The young despot was as eager as any Nero for praise, and would have gone to any lengths in his new-born desire for the approval of the greatest sage of the time. But in the Platonic theory the mind of the philosopher king must pass through a long and arduous course of training—a training whose asceticism was more than anything else likely to disgust a sensualist. Instead of turning to account Dionysius' will and power, and leaving his motives for later improvement, the two enthusiasts, Plato and Dion, began to disgust their pupil with himself and with them, by pointing out to him in constant lectures his own defects. They treated him as a schoolboy, and he saw it with injured vanity. The bulk of the Dionysian party, who viewed with jealousy the immense influence of Dion and Plato, used their opportunity to arouse distrust in the despot's mind. The personal bearing of Dion, a man of brusque and intolerant character, without any of the tact and gentleness which were the charm of Plato's manner, confirmed their whispered hints. It seemed as if he actually was scheming to reduce Dionysius to insignificance, and to usurp for himself the despotism, or hand it over to the other claimants, the sons of Aristomache. Distrust grew into jealousy, jealousy into hatred; and finally, after four months of sullen endurance, Dionysius inveigled his uncle to the quays of Ortygia, ordered him into a boat which was there lying manned, and sent him away from Syracuse. He did not, however, interfere in any way with the exile's property, or alter at all his deferential demeanour towards Plato; and it was only some months later (366 B.C.) that the philosopher, who now saw his last chance of success thwarted, was allowed to depart, under promise however that he would return when asked. He consented to this arrangement on the despot promising to recall Dion at the same time.

The leader of the opposition to Dion had been Philistus, who had been recalled to Syracuse immediately upon the accession of Dionysius II. He now became chief minister, and doubtless carried out as far as possible the traditions of the government of the late tyrant. But we have no details of the history of the seven years which intervened between the banishment of Dion, and the year 360 B.C.

At some time previous to that date Plato had once again been prevailed upon to visit Syracuse; but Dionysius had not fulfilled his promise of recalling Dion. On the contrary, he proceeded to confiscate the exile's property, declared Dion's wife Arete divorced, and gave her in marriage to one of his own courtiers, and yet more deeply roused his uncle's resentment by purposely leading his son into habits of intemperance. In despair Plato escaped for the last time from his dangerous host, and returned to Athens, 360 B.C. His departure was rendered a matter of prudence, as well as of wish, by the hostility of the mercenaries, who attributed to his influence the fact that their pay had been curtailed. They broke out into open mutiny, and actually assaulted Ortygia, being at last pacified by the concession of all their demands. The blame of the mutiny was thrown upon Heraclides, a personal friend of Dion, and long a court favourite. He was now sent into exile, and joined Dion in the Peloponnesus.

With the news of Dionysius' brutality towards his wife and family, Dion gave up his hopes of a reconciliation, and prepared to revenge his wrongs by force. Most of the years of his banishment had been passed at Athens; but he had also visited many of the notable cities of Greece, and was of sufficient influence to get together with ease a small force which collected at Corcyra, 357 B.C., ignorant of the object for which they were levied. Here they were joined by Dion, who thus found himself at the head of 800 picked troops, 1,000 Syracusan exiles, whom his name had attracted to an unknown service, and a tiny squadron of five merchant vessels. Heraclides was still busy in the Peloponnesus collecting and manning a more pretentious squadron.

To attack the power of Sysacuse within its very stronghold was an enterprise in which the mightiest armaments of Greece and Africa had repeatedly been foiled. Small wonder then that the announcement of the object of the expedition spread dismay through the scanty force. Of the 1,000 exiles not thirty undertook so great a hazard, and it was only by dint of lavish promises and persuasion that Dion could hold together the remainder of his company. And yet there was much in his favour. The despot of Syracuse was no longer a man of strong arm and stronger mind, but a drunken youth of no experience in war. The mercenaries which had been the bulwark of his father's power were mutinous. Within the walls of Ortygia there were rivals to his throne. All these dangers were to be added to the perpetual insecurity of a tyrant's tenure and the hatred which his subjects of all classes bore towards him. The cities of Sicily, from Syracuse downward, were as eager now as ever to throw off the yoke of their subjection, and the same was true of the Italian cities dependent upon Syracuse. Moreover, the crusade against Dionysius was headed by a man of character known and approved by all Hellas, and was supported by the influence, if reluctant, of Plato himself. The actual walls of Ortygia alone must see the decision of the conflict. And this Dion knew. He wasted no time in occupying a distant part of Dionysius' dominions, but steered straight from Corcyra for Sicily itself. Philistus, aware of the approaching attack, had stationed himself with a fleet off the southern shores of Italy, never dreaming that his enemy would attempt any but the ordinary coasting route to Sicily. In consequence the small squadron crossed in safety, and had already passed Cape Pachynus when a gale sprang up and drove it to the south-west. With difficulty it reached Heraclea Minoa, then under Carthaginian rule, where the governor, Synalus, received Dion with every mark of sympathy.* More welcome still was the news that Dionysius had sailed but a few days before for Italy with a fleet of eighty vessels, leaving Syracuse in charge of Timocrates. Instantly Dion moved across the island, reinforced as he went by contingents hastily got together from Agrigentum, Gela, Camarina, and the Sicel tribes; and at dawn of the third morning he occupied the Helorine Road where it crosses the Anapus. Timocrates, now in command of the whole mercenary force, occupied Ortygia on the one side of the town and Epipolæ on the other; but many of his men had moved northwards to defend Leontini, misled by the rumour that Dion would approach from that quarter. Whatever resistance he might have shown was, however, paralyzed by the atti-

---

* Dion had frequently acted as envoy of the Elder Dionysius to Carthage, which would account for his being on such friendly terms with Synalus.

tude of the Syracusans, who rose *en masse*, threw open
the gates, and placed Achradina in the hands of Dion
and his 5,000 men.   Timocrates, without waiting to be attacked, left the garrison which he commanded in Epipclæ
and fled.   The citizens met in public assembly for the
first time for nearly fifty years, and unanimously elected
Dion and his brother, Megacles, sole generals.   But to
this Dion would not assent, and twenty others were
nominated to act as colleagues of the two brothers.
Without delay the new generals assaulted and carried
Euryalus, the almost impregnable fortress of Epipolæ,
whose garrison, deserted by Timocrates, made no resistance
worthy of the name, and then turned their attention to
the capture of Ortygia.   To attempt an escalade was out
of the question.   A blockade was the sole means of re-
ducing that fortress, and a wall was accordingly at once
constructed from sea to sea across the necropolis—the
open space which lay between the islet and the walls of
Achradina and Neapolis.

   The fortress was, however, still open on the seaward
side, and seven days later Dionysius sailed once more
into the Great Harbour with his whole squadron of eighty
ships of war.   But of all Syracuse only the space within
the citadel's walls now remained to him, and revolt was
spreading amongst his dependencies, headed by Leontini.
Dionysius resorted to stratagem.   Pretending to be prepared to make terms at any cost, he requested that
envoys should visit him and settle the conditions of
peace.   The Syracusans, believing their work accomplished, gave way, as the despot had foreseen, to festivity,
and neglected the defence of the blockade wall.   His
mercenaries, choosing their opportunity, suddenly sallied
from Ortygia, and in a moment carried the whole wall,
which they proceeded to demolish; and Dion only succeeded in driving them back and recovering his position
after a furious battle, and at the imminent risk of his
own life.   Soon afterwards the appearance of Heraclides,
with a fleet of eighteen vessels, presently reinforced by
sixty which the Syracusans themselves equipped, deprived Dionysius of his command of the sea, and his

consequent ability to obtain regular supplies. The return of Philistus with his fleet for a moment relieved him ; but in a general engagement which followed, the flotilla under Heraclides, sixty strong, completely defeated, and for the most part destroyed, that of Philistus of similar strength ; and, more disastrous than all, the latter officer, the despot's one able adviser, was captured and brutally put to death. The reduction of Ortygia became now only a question of time.

Unfortunately for Dion, he now found a rival in the person of Heraclides, and dissension broke out in the ranks of the besiegers. The arrogance of Dion and his relationship to the house of Dionysius combined to make him an object of distrust to the citizens, who did not care to fight for one who might use his victory only to make himself their master. On the other hand, Heraclides was a man of winning, even of insidious, manners, fresh from the glory of his recent naval victory, and what was more important than all, not a member of the hated Dionysian family. The Syracusans had lately voted him admiral, and Dion, complaining that such a course, adopted without consulting himself, interfered with his own authority, had requested the citizens to cancel their vote. They did so ; whereupon Dion himself proposed and carried the appointment of Heraclides. He succeeded indeed in gratifying his own pride, but he drew upon himself the decided enmity of his rival, and gave fresh colour to the charge of aiming at the *tyrannis*. Dionysius, apprised of these matters, turned them to the best account. He spread treacherous reports through the city, compromising still more the character of Dion ; and he caused letters to be written in which he invited Dion to take his place as despot, offering to retire on those terms. These letters were publicly read by order of Dion ; but rather increased than allayed the prevalent suspicions. Heraclides now put himself forward as the direct opponent of Dion. He thwarted his wishes in every possible way, and finally secured his dismissal, with the further injustice that the arrears due to Dion's troops should not be paid. With such rancour did he follow up his revenge, that he induced the citizens even to attack the small force of Dion as he led it out of Syracuse; and it found shelter at last in Leontini, 366 B.C.

Some time previous to this crisis, Dionysius had escaped from Ortygia to Locri, leaving that fortress and its garrison in charge of his son Apollocrates. Lack of provisions had almost induced the latter to surrender, when the quarrels of his opponents, resulting in a less vigorous watch upon the seas, allowed a large convoy of provisions and reinforcements under Nypsius to reach Ortygia from Locri, and thus placed him once more in a position to maintain the place. But Nypsius took further advantage of the quarrel. A slight success gained by Heraclides' fleet over the vessels of the convoy, though occurring too late to prevent the relief of Ortygia, yet threw the Syracusans once more into a condition of extravagant confidence, in the midst of which Nypsius sallied out, carried the blockading wall, burst into Neapolis and Tyche, and finally into Achradina, thus destroying at a blow the labours of months. He let loose his mercenaries upon the city, which they plundered right and left, until the Syracusans, in despair, despatched an express to Leontini, entreating Dion to forget and forgive, and once again to come to the rescue of their city. With noble patriotism Dion complied, and moved at once towards Syracuse, arriving at Epipolæ by daybreak. Here he was met by orders from Heraclides, forbidding his nearer approach. The withdrawal of Nypsius to Ortygia at the close of his day's pillage had restored the courage of the Syracusans, who once more remembered their party jealousies. The next day they had reason to repent their haste. Nypsius renewed his attack, and this time he spared nothing. The town was deluged with bloodshed, and the mercenaries were ordered to fire it in all directions. In the midst of these horrors, Dion led his troops down from Epipolæ, and falling upon the mercenaries while the latter were scattered and disorganized, he drove them back to Ortygia. Then, rebuilding the wall of blockade, and quenching the flames, he set himself once more to reduce the fortress. Heraclides, to whom were due all the recent disasters, he not only pardoned but even defended from the resentment of the citizens, securing his appointment as admiral while he himself resumed the supreme command of the land army.

Fresh dissensions soon broke out. Heraclides, sailing off on the pretence of attacking Dionysius at Locri, took the opportunity to inflame his crews against Dion and to make a secret treaty with Dionysius. The mediator was Pharax, lieutenant of the despot's forces, and he succeeded at least in thus frustrating the purpose of the expedition, although the furious opposition of the majority of the Syracusans prevented Heraclides from carrying out his engagement on his return. Shortly afterwards Pharax landed near Agrigentum, probably by arrangement with Heraclides; and the latter moved his fleet southwards, professing his intention of executing a joint attack upon the enemy in conjunction with the land force under Dion. But the fleet, instead of coming into action, suffered Dion to commence his attack, and then sailed away with all speed to Syracuse in the hope of seizing the city and barring the return of the land force and its general. The latter was beaten off, but was able by the rapidity of his return to frustrate this second act of treachery. Heraclides, finding himself thwarted on all sides, at length withdrew his opposition, and shortly after Apollocrates surrendered. He was allowed to retire with so much property as he could put on board five vessels. Ortygia, with its docks, arsenals, and stores, remained in the hands of Dion after a struggle of two years (355 B.C.).

It was now time for Dion to fulfil the promises of liberty which he had made to the Syracusans on his first return. He had expelled the House of Dionysius, and was master of its military resources. The Syracusans were eager to commence at once the demolition of the 'Bastile of Syracuse.' But Dion declined to give the word. He still nursed his philosophic dreams; and the freedom which he intended to give the city was not that of an Athenian democracy. The Platonics found their

ideal government in Sparta, where the ancient monarchy
existed side by side with a scarcely less ancient oligarchy
and a more modern element of democracy.   This had
been from time immemorial the polity of a State whose
conservatism and solidarity were unique in Hellas, and
under such a polity Sparta had retained for centuries the
position of leader of Greece.   On these lines the liberty of
Syracuse was now to be organized, and the ideal monarch,
the philosopher-king, was to be Dion himself.   But, freed
from the actual presence of Dionysius, the Syracusans
laughed at that philosophy to which they had once looked
for deliverance, and turned themselves to anticipations of
the freedom which had been their own after the overthrow
of Thrasybulus.   They expected Dion to dismantle
Ortygia, to disband his forces, to resign his office of
general, and to submit himself as a citizen to the popular
judgment of his fellows.   He did nothing of all this.   He
transferred, indeed, his family and property to his original
dwelling outside the citadel ; but he still kept under arms
a force probably little inferior in numbers to that of
Dionysius, and made no sign of surrendering his post.
The people murmured, and found a leader in Heraclides,
who could now veil his hostility to Dion under the credit-
able guise of patriotism.   Dion saw himself gradually
drifting away from his high popularity, while Heraclides
took his place in the confidence of the people.   His
jealousy at length got the better of himself and his philosophy.   He caused his rival to be assassinated, and in so
doing declared himself despot.   Too late the people saw
how little trust could be placed in any of the kin of
Dionysius.   A reign of terror set in.   The first act of
lawlessness made easier any after deeds ; and within
twelve months of his victory, Dion the Liberator was
known only as Dion the Tyrant.

He paid the penalty of his mistake in the manner of
most despots.   Callippus the Athenian, himself, too,
something of a disciple of Plato, long the host of Dion
during his exile and now his confidant, contrived a widespread conspiracy.   The trustfulness of Dion towards his
' own particular friend ' enabled Callippus to associate as

he pleased with known malcontents on the pretence of dis-
covering their secrets by a feigned sympathy.   Arete, the
despot's wife, more quick-sighted than her husband,
charged him with treachery, and he swore his innocence
by the most awful oaths.   On the festival of the Coreia*
he contrived that the garrisons and gates should all be in
the hands of the conspirators, and, surrounding Dion's
house, had him stabbed to death by a band of young men
who represented themselves as coming on a matter of
business (353 B.C.).

* So called from Core (' the maiden '); *i.e.*, Proserpina, in whose honour it was
held.

CHAPTER X.

The Liberation of Timoleon.

Despotism of Callippus—Hicetas heads a Rising—Nysæus seizes Ortygia—Intrigues of the Dionysian Claimants—Miserable Condition of Sicily and Magna Græcia—Dionysius returns to Ortygia—The Syracusans Appeal to Corinth—Early Life of Timoleon—He accepts the Post of Liberator—Treachery of Hicetas—Timoleon eludes the Carthaginians at Rhegium—Lands at Tauromenium, and defeats Hicetas at Adranum—Dionysius surrenders Ortygia and retires to Corinth—The Corinthians send fresh Succours—Hicetas and Mago besiege Neon in Ortygia—Mago withdraws, and Timoleon drives out Hicetas—He destroys the Fortifications of Ortygia, and refounds Syracuse—Expels other Tyrants, and defeats the Carthaginians at Crimesus—Puts to Death Hicetas and Mamercus, and concludes Peace with Carthage—He lays down his Command—Later Years, and Death—Rapid Recovery of the Sicilian Towns.

BUT this last murder brought no better fortune to the unhappy city. Callippus made the usual promises of liberty, and for a few hours posed as a tyrannicide. He soon threw off the disguise, and in his turn declared himself despot. He imprisoned the wife and sister of Dion, and established himself firmly by dint of force. The mercenaries whom Dionysius II. had left behind him, and who had it seems passed into the service of Dion, now transferred their swords to Callippus. The enormities of the tyrant soon roused open resistance, and Syracuse became once more the battle-ground of rival factions. One revolt failed, and the defeated party, led by Hicetas, a friend of Dion, took refuge in Leontini. A second was more successful. Hipparinus and Nysæus, sons of Dionysius I. and Aristomache, headed a rising and seized the town while Callippus was absent with his troops at Catana, probably following up his recent advantage at Leontini. How insufferable the despotism of Callippus must have been may best be judged from the fact that members of the House of Dionysius could now find sufficient support to recover the city of their father, 352 B.C.

Callippus was forced to content himself with the despotism of Catana. Hicetas established himself as despot of Leontini; at Syracuse things grew worse and worse. The city was divided between three parties who schemed and quarrelled and fought without ceasing, and converted the various quarters of the town into camps, its streets into battle-fields. Hipparinus headed the party who favoured the younger branch of the family of Dionysius, the children of the Syracusan Aristomache; and he was so far the superior that he had possession of Ortygia. Against him were arrayed a second party who schemed to restore Dionysius himself. Against both these struggled the party of liberty. At Leontini, Hicetas watched an opportunity to return. Callippus at Catana could have been no peaceful neighbour, and was succeeded by Mamercus, as great a ruffian as himself. Murders and bloodshed prevailed everywhere. The wife and sister of Dion, set free by their son and nephew Hipparinus, were murdered by their pretended friend Hicetas. Hipparinus himself was slain in a fit of drunkenness, and his place occupied by Nysæus. The temples of the Gods, the tombs of the dead, were neglected or violated. The ruin wrought by Nypsius remained unrepaired. Of all the wide dominions of the Syracuse of twenty years before, nothing now remained to her. Leptines was despot of Apollonia, Nicodemus of Centoripe, Apolloniades of Agyrium, and other towns shared the common lot. Nothing is known of the condition of the cities of the southern and western parts of Sicily; but it is known that Carthage, awaking at last from her apathy, was gradually encroaching upon the island, and that bands of Campanian mercenaries roamed at will, desolating the land, and substituting for the commerce and culture of Hellenism the barbarism of the Oscans. Plato (or the author of the letters attributed to that philosopher), writing from Athens, prophesies the speedy disappearance of even the Greek tongue from Sicily, and the swallowing up of Greek despotism and Greek democracy alike in the power of Carthaginians and Campanians. He implored the factions to be reconciled while there was still time, and bade them form a triple monarchy, like the double kingship of Sparta, in which the male descendants of Doris, of Aristomache, and of Dion, should rule side by side. In Magna Græcia things were no better. That Locri which the Elder Dionysius had advanced to be the first city of Southern Italy was now desolated by the brutalities and cruelties of his son within, and by the growing pressure of the Italian tribes, Lucanians and Bruttians, without. Nothing but the sword maintained Dionysius II. in his mother's State, and no relief came until 346 B.C., when he once more seized Ortygia, and transferred his tyranny to Syracuse anew. Then the Locrians rose and reasserted their liberties. They seized the wife and children of Dionysius, and revenged upon them the despot's crimes. For weeks these captives afforded a spectacle of insult and agony to their infuriated enemies, while beyond the walls the fleet and forces of Dionysius tried all that prayers and bribes and violence could do to rescue them. They died under their tortures, and Dionysius returned to avenge his ill-success upon the Sicilians. And now Carthage, confident of an easy conquest of the distracted island, set herself to reduce it in earnest. In utter despair the Syracusans sent a piteous appeal to their metropolis and entreated Corinth to rescue them if it might be so.

The embassy reached Corinth at a time (344 B.C.) shortly after the termination of the Sacred War by Philip of Macedon, when Greece lay in a state of apprehensive quietude, fearful of making any movement which might rouse his jealousy. Corinth was therefore free from any activity at home, and glad of the opportunity to engage without risk in the affairs of Sicily. A vote of assistance was immediately passed, and the chance nomination of one of the assembled citizens conferred the command upon Timoleon.

The son of noble parents, a man of tried bravery and wonderful gentleness, Timoleon had for nearly twenty years lived the life of a recluse at his country house, tormented by the *erinnys* of his brother's murder and his mother's curse. In the year 366 B.C., Corinth was engaged as an ally of Sparta and Athens in resisting the growing power of Thebes,.to whom, with the battle of Leuctra, had passed the hegemony of Greece. The Athenians had, despite the fact of the alliance, formed a plan for surprising the town of Corinth, and though timely warning of the intended treachery enabled the Corinthians to put themselves on their guard, yet the imminency of the risk induced them to establish a permanent garrison of mercenary troops, 400 in number, who were put under the command of Timophanes, brother of Timoleon. Since the fall of Psammetichus, the last of the Cypselid despots, 581 B.C., the town had been ruled by a moderate oligarchy, who, despite the security of their tenure, did not care to arm the populace as a garrison. Their caution did not benefit them, for Timophanes at once threw off all restraint and established himself as despot by·wholesale murder, finding his instrument in the mercenaries under him. In vain did Timoleon reason with his brother, whose life he had once saved at the peril of his own,[*] and finding entreaties vain, he adopted a terrible course. Taking into his confidence the brother of the tyrant's wife, and one or perhaps two other friends, he visited the usurper in the Acrocorinthus,[†] and, after again pleading fruitlessly for the freedom of the city, stood by while his allies cut down Timophanes. Men heard of the deed with mingled relief and horror ;[‡] his mother cursed him, and he withdrew, a broken-hearted man, from all intercourse with the world.

His appointment to the command against Dionysius

---

[*] In a battle between the Argives and the troops of Argos and Cleone. The date is unknown.

[†] The citadel or acropolis of Corinth.

[‡] To kill a tyrant was an act of virtue ; but to shed the blood of a kinsman was an inexpiable crime in Grecian eyes.

9

and Carthage came to him as a glad distraction from his own thoughts. It was a forlorn hope in the eyes of all men ; and the Corinthians told him as he departed that if he succeeded they would regard him as justified in his crime ; if he failed, as receiving heaven's chastisement for it. Their diminished resources prevented them from furnishing him with any adequate force. Timoleon himself was too poor to equip more than seven triremes. His entire force, not counting one or two distinguished Corinthians who accompanied him as volunteers, amounted only to ten vessels and 1,200 men, mostly discharged mercenaries lately serving on the Phocian side in the Sacred War, and branded with the charge of sacrilege for their participation in the plundering of the great temple of Delphi.

Before he could sail, there reached Corinth an embassy from Hicetas, countermanding the request of the Syracusans, to which he had been a party, that assistance should be sent. That despot had so strengthened himself at Leontini, that he had forces sufficient to face Dionysius in the field, and upon him the Syracusans mainly relied for the moment. But he had designs of his own which would be hindered by the appearance of a Corinthian force. He aimed at seizing Syracuse for himself by the help of the Carthaginians, who were now close at hand. Accordingly, having now matured his arrangements with the latter, he sent word to Corinth that the delay in the appearance of any succours from that city had compelled him to enter into alliance with Carthage, who declined to allow the interference of any Corinthian armament. Timoleon saw through the pretext, and knew that he had now lost his only ally in Sicily ; but none the less he hurried to the scene of action, and the omens that greeted him at Delphi and elsewhere, marked him out as the chosen instrument of Ceres and Proserpina for the delivery of their island.

Arrived at Rhegium, Timoleon found further progress barred by the presence of a Carthaginian fleet of twenty ships, having on board an envoy from Hicetas. That despot was now in possession of the whole of Syracuse with the exception of Ortygia, where he kept Dionysius closely blockaded by the help of the Carthaginian main fleet under Hanno. His envoy therefore declared that, as the surrender of Dionysius was now a foregone conclusion, the presence of Timoleon was needless, and his return to Corinth necessary, inasmuch as the Carthaginians declined to allow him to land in Sicily. Seeming to assent, Timoleon bade the envoy explain the matter in public assembly before the Rhegines, where he himself attended after giving secret orders to his crews to watch their opportunity, and quietly put across one by one. The Carthaginians, deeming the matter settled, paid no further attention to the movements of the Corinthian vessels, which made the passage safely to Tauromenium; and when the assembly, at the close of the envoy's address, looked around for Timoleon to reply, they learnt that he too had quietly slipped away and joined his men.

But though he had at length reached Sicily, Timoleon found his position precarious. Tauromenium, though a strong fortress, was not of sufficient importance to give him any positive aid, and he had no other allies in the island. Suddenly there reached him a summons from Adranum, a Sicelo-Greek town, forty-two miles inland, where a party quarrel had ended in the appeal of one faction to Hicetas, the other to Timoleon. He marched thither at once, and arrived near the town—a small place, but of importance as the holy town of the Sicel God Adranus—on the same evening as did Hicetas. The latter, unaware of the vicinity of his enemy, allowed his men to bivouac; and Timoleon, taking them by surprise, completely defeated them. The Sicels accepted his victory as a sign of the favour of their God. He was admitted into the town, and in a short time received the adhesion of many small Sicel communities and the more important alliance of Mamercus, despot of Catana.

With an army thus reinforced to the number of 2,000 men, Timoleon marched at once to Syracuse. His arrival found Dionysius on the point of capitulating to Hicetas, and it averted the passing of Ortygia into the hands of a despot as inhuman as its former master. To surrender to Hicetas meant certain death for Dionysius; to surrender to Timoleon might secure personal safety and would at any rate balk Hicetas of his prize. Within a few hours a Corinthian garrison of 400 men under Neon passed into the fortress, where the mercenaries, 2,000 in number, at once embraced the cause of Timoleon; and Dionysius, with some small portion of his property and money, was received into Timoleon's camp. He was immediately dismissed to Corinth, where he lived as a private citizen for the remaining years of his life, passing his time in drinking and idleness; and on his death, he left behind him a favourite example to all time of retribution slow to come but sure. 'Dionysius at Corinth'* became a proverb for an uncrowned king. Asked once in what way his Platonic studies had benefited him, he had the spirit to reply that they had at least taught him how to bear his changed fortunes. Another explanation of his passive endurance was the fact that any undue activity on his part would certainly bring upon him the sword of justice, which he knew was only stayed, not sheathed, in his favour.†

The arrival of Dionysius in Corinth, as proof of the marvellous success of Timoleon, led to the instant equipment of a fresh force of 2,200 foot and horse, which were despatched forthwith and safely reached Thurii. Here a large Carthaginian force barred their progress; but, marching across Bruttium, they reached Rhegium, found the strait unguarded, and so crossed without molestation to Messana, which town at once declared for Timoleon.

After the occupation of Ortygia, with all its stores (including arms for 70,000 men, laid up probably by Dionysius the Elder), Timoleon had withdrawn the remainder of his small army to Adranum. Hicetas now laid fresh siege to Ortygia, and called in the aid of the united fleet and army of the Carthaginians, to the number of 60,000 men and 150 ships, under Mago. Finding that the blockade was rendered futile, owing to the continued

---

* Διονύσιος ἐν Κορίνθῳ.

† There is an improbable story that he opened a school at Corinth; but he is known to have been too well off, and was presumably too indolent, for such a course.

arrival of blockade-runners from Catana, Hicetas persuaded Mago to co-operate with him in an attack on that town. No sooner had they departed, than Neon sallied out of Ortygia and captured Achradina, which he at once united to the citadel by walls; and before the absent forces could be recalled from Catana, Timoleon descended to the coast, reinforced by the new arrivals from Corinth, and seized the Olympieum. This reverse, which practically annihilated the possibility of a successful blockade, aroused the suspicions of Mago, who knew the character of Hicetas too well to trust him. His suspicions grew into alarm; and he at length drew off his entire force by night. Dawn of day saw Timoleon advance to the storming of the Carthaginian camp, which he found deserted. He now arranged for a threefold assault upon the three portions of the city which remained still in the hands of Hicetas. He himself attacked Epipolæ, the strongest position, from the steep southern side; the new Corinthian reinforcements assaulted it from the less difficult northern slope; while Neon and the garrison in Ortygia and Achradina attacked Tyche and Neapolis. Hicetas was driven out with slight resistance and fled to Leontini, leaving the entire city in the hands of Timoleon.

Timoleon had accomplished what no Greek invader had ever done before at Syracuse; he now achieved a greater victory still, and one unique in the annals of Greek history. At one blow he might have made himself despot of the city which had been the victim of so much self-seeking, and which even the philosophic Dion could not endure to give up. Timoleon rased at once the walls of Ortygia, and blotted out the stronghold of Syracusan, even of Sicilian, *tyrannis*. On the spot he built in its stead halls of justice. Then he turned to the graver problem of restoring the fallen city and healing the wounds of the past years of misery. He summoned back to their homes all exiles, and invited colonists from Greece, whose advent under Corinthian auspices marked the second founding of the city. By these measures 10,000 new inhabitants were enrolled, many of them men of wealth.   To accommodate them, the lands and houses of Syracuse were sold by auction, and the money thus obtained served to relieve the miserably impoverished remnant of the old citizens.   Two native Corinthians, Cephalus and Dionysius, men of high estimation and character, came as commissioners to revise the constitution ; and they revived the laws of Diocles, which had been so briefly exercised on their original institution.* No details are known as to their character, save that they were democratical.

But the restoration of Syracusan liberty was but a part of the task to which Timoleon had bound himself. After some months of quietude, during which he was busied with the settlement of the new colonists, he moved against Leontini, Apollonia, and other cities. Hicetas professed instant submission, and was for the moment spared ; Leptines of Apollonia was deposed and sent away to Corinth.   Timoleon then returned to his work at Syracuse, despatching his troops to the west of the island to gather pay and plunder from the Carthaginian province.   Hicetas was at the moment negotiating for fresh Carthaginian assistance, and the news of the foray into Western Sicily came just at the right moment to support his appeal.   Moreover, the Carthaginians were smarting under the ignominy of the recent retreat of Mago from Syracuse—a retreat all the more vexing as until then no Carthaginian army had ever been admitted within the walls.   They revenged themselves by crucifying the dead body of Mago, who committed suicide to avoid a more painful death, and then turned their whole energy to organising a fresh invasion of the island.

In the spring of 340 B.C, Hamilcar and Hasdrubal landed at Lilybæum with 70,000 men and 2,000 war chariots, and a fleet of 500 ships of war and twice that number of transports to co-operate with them by sea. The army moved eastward upon Syracuse, and the news of its approach spread panic amongst the new settlers, to whom Carthaginian warfare was a matter of hearsay only.   Timoleon could levy only 13,000 men of all arms,

* See above, p. 83.

including those troops which had lately been raiding beyond the Halycus; and of this small force, 1,000 mercenaries, prompted by their commander Thrasius, deserted on the road and marched back to Syracuse. With difficulty could Timoleon retain the residue of his men, who marched on as if to certain death. Their gloomy forebodings seemed confirmed by the appearance of a train of mules laden with parsley, a plant largely used in funeral ceremonies. Timoleon's ready wit averted the evil omen. He seized a handful of the leaves, and bound them as a chaplet on his brow, reminding his men that it was also the garland of the conqueror at their own Isthmian games. The troops recovered their spirits, and at early dawn heard the Carthaginian host, six times as numerous, fording the swampy stream of the Crimesus* below them. It was now May, and the mist which lay along the valley prevented the invading army from seeing their enemies, even had they been prepared to find any opposition so near to their own territories. The chariots had already crossed, and behind them the chosen Carthaginian infantry, including the 2,500 of the sacred band.† But the bulk of the army, the mixed mercenary troops, were still on the farther bank, and thus the charge of Timoleon's cavalry had to deal only with a portion of their foes. His cavalry could effect little, however, against the solid wall of chariots, though the latter were, from the hilly nature of the ground, unable to come into real action. Still, the Carthaginian army was in a measure disordered by the sudden attack, and ill prepared for the charge of the Grecian hoplites led by Timoleon in person. The marvellous good fortune which had always waited upon their leader had brought the Greeks to regard him as the favourite of heaven, and they followed him now with enthusiastic courage. The battle was terrible. That of

* The battle was fought about the head waters of this stream, which rises in the difficult mountainous country on the direct road between Panormus and Selinus. It was thus well within the Carthaginian reservation, where they would expect no resistance.

† Composed, like the similar body at Thebes, of picked young warriors, so arranged that each had at his side his dearest friend. They were the flower of the native aristocracy.

Leuctra alone could equal it for the obstinacy of the hand-to-hand struggle. Spears were useless against the mail of the native Carthaginians, and it became a struggle of the short dagger-like sword. A terrific storm of hail and rain, accompanied by thunder and lightning, now burst upon the combatants. It affected the Greeks little, as it beat only upon their backs, but it soon threw the Carthaginian ranks into disorder. What kept the chariots still inactive we do not know. They rendered at any rate no assistance, and when the front line of infantry turned at last to fly, they found themselves checked by the still advancing numbers of their own mercenaries. But once began, the rout soon extended. The whole army of Carthage was beaten back to Lilybæum, leaving behind 15,000 prisoners and 10,000 dead, including, it is said, the entire Sacred Band. The booty of their camp, with its gold and silver plate, and the costly panoplies of the native troops, was enormous, and did more to recoup at once the impoverishment of Syracuse than any of Timoleon's more peaceful measures (340 B.C.).

Hicetas and Mamercus, who had been unable to join the Carthaginian army before its defeat, were now isolated. They appealed once more for help, and in this or the next year (339 B.C.) a mercenary army under Gisco* appeared off the north coast of the island. One or two successes were gained by the two despots over detachments commanded by officers of Timoleon, and they were now joined by Messana, which had been seized by a tyrant named Hippo. Hicetas even undertook a raid into the territory of Syracuse, but on his return he was defeated with the loss of 1,000 men by a mere handful of cavalry under Timoleon at the river Damurias; and on the appearance of the Syracusan army before Leontini shortly afterwards the garrison surrendered the town and its despot. The Syracusans put him to death, with his whole family, in revenge for the murder of Aristomache and Arete.† A little later Mamercus and Gisco were defeated on the river Abolus; and the Carthaginians,

* He is called the son of Hanno, possibly the admiral mentioned on p. 131. He appears to have been banished for his father's ill success, and was now recalled to take the command.

† See p. 127.

giving up the struggle, sued for peace. The river Halycus was once more made the boundary between the Grecian and Carthaginian territories, and a special clause stipulated for the absolute freedom of all the Greek cities (339 B.C.).

Mamercus now applied to the Lucanians for aid, but the surrender of Catana by its garrison to Timoleon compelled him to fly to Hippo at Messana. The town was at once besieged. Hippo, endeavouring to escape by sea, was caught and put to death in the theatre before the assembled people of all ages. Mamercus surrendered to Timoleon, who carried him to Syracuse, where he defended himself in vain before the assembly, and was executed as a brigand. In rapid succession fell the few remaining despots in the island. The various settlements of foreign mercenaries were expelled, and by the year 337 B.C., all Sicily east of the Halycus was once more Hellenic and free.

Timoleon returned to Syracuse and at once laid down his command. Like Cæsar, he could say, *Veni, vidi, vici;* and he could further add *vixi.* No shadow of suspicion had ever crossed his path, and now he ended his days still the first and best-beloved citizen of the State which he had restored, and no less honoured throughout Sicily than in Syracuse. He sent for his family from Corinth, and lived upon an estate voted to him by the people. He was attacked with blindness in the last months of his life, but none the less shared in all the public business of the State, and his opinion was seldom disputed. Once only did he meet with any ingratitude. Laphystius and Demænetus ventured to attack him on petty grounds, and he insisted on having the matter tried in public in the usual way. His acquittal was, of course, a foregone conclusion; but he expressed his gratification at being thus able to prove how entirely he was on a level with the meanest of his fellow-citizens. He died in 337 or 336 B.C., and his funeral was magnificent in the extreme. His tomb was known as the Timoleontium, and his memory was honoured with public games and contests as that of a hero.

Before his death, he had seen the prosperity of Sicily rise anew. Colonists from all parts of Greece, leaving the sphere of Macedonian supremacy, crowded to the old cities of Sicily. Gela, Agrigentum and Camarina attained once more to something of their ancient opulence and grandeur, and the whole of the Hellenic portion of the island shared in their good fortune. The land which had been a desert at the time of Timoleon's first arrival became once more the garden of the Mediterranean; and it may have owed something of its prosperity to the depression which still weighed down the cities of Magna Græcia, where the Lucanians and Bruttians continually pushed their ascendancy. Increase of power and opulence brought with it the usual disturbances, and within a very few years of the death of Timoleon even Syracuse was again in the hands of an oligarchy. We know nothing of the process of the change, only that the oligarchy was close in the extreme, limited either in fact or in name to 600. Corinthian influence coming in with the new settlers may have contributed to the change; but the history of these later events belongs to the time of Agathocles.

CHAPTER XI.

Agathocles.

His Origin and Early Life—Military Successes—Is banished in the Italian War — His Return — Expulsion of Sosistratus — Again banished and recalled—He arms the Rabble and sacks Syracuse —Is proclaimed Autocrat—Collusion of the Carthaginian General— Acrotatus commands the Exiles—His Conduct and Flight—Dissolution of the League and Aggrandisement of Agathocles—Proceedings of Carthage against Hamilcar — Dinocrates heads the Exiles, who obtain Assistance from Carthage—Arrival of Hamilcar Gisco —Battle of Ecnomus and Siege of Syracuse—Agathocles prepares to quit Syracuse—He lands in Africa—His Reasons—He burns his Ships—Defeats the Carthaginians—Hamilcar raises the Siege of Syracuse — The Libyans join Agathocles — Defeat and Death of Hamilcar—Agrigentum heads the revolted Sicilians—Mutiny and Second Victory of the African Army—Arrival of Ophellas—History of Cyrene—Treason of Bomilcar—Agathocles revisits Sicily—Defeat of Archagathus—Return of Agathocles—His Flight—Cruelties in Sicily—Italian and other Wars—Death and Character.

THE name of Agathocles, like that of so many of the great names of history, was surrounded from an early date with an atmosphere of prodigy. In simple fact he was the son of Carcinus, an exile from Rhegium, who had fled to Thermæ, at that time under Carthaginian dominion, and there practised the trade of a potter. When Timoleon, after the battle of Crimesus, bestowed the freedom of Syracuse upon all who chose to demand it, Carcinus enrolled himself as a citizen and migrated with his son, now about twenty-two years of age, to Syracuse, where both continued to practise the father's trade. To these bare details legend added that Carcinus, warned by dreams and by the Delphian oracle that the child yet to be born would bring mighty calamities upon

Carthage and Sicily alike, had exposed Agathocles at his birth, and left him to perish. His mother, however, a native of Thermæ, had contrived to rescue him, and had placed him under the care of her brother, with whom he remained seven years. His beauty and growth then attracted the notice of his father, whose admiration encouraged the mother to reveal the child's identity, and so to secure for him his rights.*

Agathocles was already infamous for his vices when he came to reside at Syracuse. Here he found a patron in Damas,† one of the leading citizens, who was the means not only of enriching him, but of advancing him to public notice. In a war arising out of the old jealousy between Syracuse and Agrigentum,‡ Damas, commander of the Syracusan army, appointed his favourite to be captain of a division. Already distinguished for his size and strength, Agathocles gained in the war the further reputation of headlong daring and high courage. At its close he so improved his opportunities as to become a popular leader, for which his audacity and fluency well fitted him; and on the death of Damas he married the latter's widow, thus succeeding to a large property and to his late patron's position.

Some time after, the Crotoniates,§ being harassed by the Bruttii, appealed to Syracuse, and a strong force was despatched to their assistance under Heraclides and Sosistratus, both men of infamous lives and leading oligarchs. The known democratic spirit of Agathocles, now serving as a chiliarch by special appointment of the people, prejudiced the generals against him to such a degree that they withheld from him the due rewards of his indisputable courage and bravery. He retorted by accusing them of aiming at the despotism; but his warnings being unheeded, Sosistratus carried out his design, became virtual master of Syracuse,‖ and compelled Agathocles to go into exile. The latter formed the plan of

* Compare the story of Cyrus the Great.
† Or Damasco.
‡ Justin says Ætna was the belligerent town..
§ Others say the Campani. At any rate, it was an Italiot war.
‖ It is not known whether Sosistratus became despot, or merely subverted the democracy in favour of the Six Hundred.

seizing Crotona, where, as the bravest soldier in the army lately sent to the town's assistance, he might reasonably hope for success. The plot failed, however, perhaps owing to the action of the Sosistratid party, and Agathocles fled to Tarentum, where he offered his services as a mercenary. Here, too, his very bravery aroused distrust, and he was again banished as guilty of revolutionary designs.

About that time Sosistratus laid siege to Rhegium. Agathocles at once offered his services to the Rhegines in the hopes of thwarting the author of his exile. It seems he succeeded, for the next we hear is that Sosistratus was banished from Syracuse and Agathocles recalled. The absence of the former in Italy, and the activity of the latter—always, of course, in the interests of the democracy—probably gave to the Syracusans at once the courage and the opportunity to recover their liberties. The Six Hundred were overthrown, and many of their supporters driven with them into exile.

As usual, however, the expulsion of so many influential citizens produced only further troubles. Had the democracy been content with the banishment of Sosistratus and a few only of his most active partisans, the remainder might have remained quiescent. As it was, they were ejected in large numbers, and being all men of position and well connected, they found ready audience and sympathy amongst the Greek cities—with oligarchic States as being themselves oligarchs, with democracies perhaps as offering a means of humbling the pride of Syracuse. Moreover, the Carthaginians, ever desirous of an occasion for fresh interference and eager to revenge themselves on Syracuse for their defeat at Crimesus, saw their opportunity in playing off one party against the other, and assisted the exiles, though we do not know to what extent. A long and dubious war followed, of which we know virtually nothing. We are told, indeed, that Agathocles was the moving spirit at Syracuse, and that he upheld the democracy alike as a private citizen and when entrusted with commands in the field, especially distinguishing himself by the manner in which he drew off his men from an unsuccessful attempt to surprise Gela by night. That town was garrisoned by Sosistratus, who was warned of the attempted surprise in time to meet the Syracusans, and coop them up in a narrow gateway. Agathocles, himself wounded in seven places, ordered his buglers to pass along the wall in opposite directions, and there give the customary signal for advance. The Geloans, hearing the signals and expecting a fresh attack in two opposite quarters, ceased their pursuit of Agathocles' force, and allowed him to draw it off in safety.

But despite his services he become an object of distrust to the Syracusans. The democracy remembered that the despot usually reached his aims by means of demagogy, and they did not forget the open attempts of Agathocles to establish himself at Crotona and Tarentum. Rival leaders of the popular party would endeavour to rid themselves of so formidable an opponent, and eventually Acestorides, a Corinthian,* at the time in command of the army, plotted the assassination of Agathocles. He gave him orders to leave the city, and placed men in ambush to despatch him on the road, neither impeachment nor open assault being likely to succeed. Agathocles dressed in his own armour a slave who was attacked and killed, while the real object of attack escaped and collected amongst the Sicel tribes an army sufficiently large to alarm both Greeks and Carthaginians. Indiscriminately attacking both, he forced them to come to terms with one another in order the more successfully to resist himself. The exiled partisans of Sosistratus were accordingly recalled, and peace was made with Carthage. Sosistratus and Heraclides were thus disarmed and the Carthaginians disposed of.

Agathocles could now direct his whole force against Syracuse. Supported by the hill-tribes, and in particular by Morgantine, he captured Leontini, shut up the Syracusans within their walls, and even laid siege to that city. Intestine feud prevented any united effort within

---

* Possibly a soldier of Timoleon's army, or sent, like that general, to act on behalf of Syracuse.

the walls, and an appeal was made to Carthage. A garrison, under Hamilcar, was thrown into Syracuse; but Agathocles won their commander over by lavish promises,* and the citizens, finding their pretended allies of no use, bought off the threatened assault by again admitting Agathocles within the walls, upon his solemn affirmation that he would make no attempt to subvert the government.

His return only intensified the bitterness of the factions within the city. Calling himself 'Patron of the Democracy,' he did his utmost to weaken the oligarchic party, now restored by the recall of the Sosistratid exiles. The latter constituted the Six Hundred, and were led by a handful of the extreme aristocracy. But democrats and oligarchs alike were divided into cliques, each with a separate aim and each hostile to the rest. Agathocles' studied moderation disarmed suspicion.† The Syracusans appointed him supreme commander and guardian of the peace until the different factions could be brought to agreement.

It seems that his action now led to the exile of a large number of citizens, who betook themselves to Herbita, a Sicel town of the north-west, and there collected a force for war. Fortune favoured Agathocles. On pretence of resisting the exiles he collected his Sicel allies from Morgantine and elsewhere, and gathered about him all the worst class of citizens to whom a revolution might bring gain. This force he stationed in readiness at the Timoleontium, and invited to a conference at that spot Pisarchus and Diocles, leaders of the oligarchy. On their arrival with forty of their supporters he had them all arrested, declaring that they came commissioned by the Six Hundred to seize him. His troops took up the cue, and demanded vengeance.

---

* It seems that Agathocles promised to aid Hamilcar in his attempt to make himself independent of Carthage, or its despot. It was not unlikely that the Carthaginians should aid the Sosistratids again; more probable still that they should transfer their assistance to Agathocles, consistently with their policy of encouraging despotism at the expense of democracy. The chronology cannot be determined.

† It is probable that he purposely fomented the feuds which he professed to allay.

Agathocles threw off all disguise, and let his men loose to plunder the property of the oligarchs. For two days the town was a scene of murder and robbery. On the third day the surviving oligarchs, and such other citizens as were likely to be dangerous, were summoned before the 'Patron of Democracy,' who put some to death and banished the rest, amongst whom was one Dinocrates. Then, declaring that he had 'purged the State,' he laid aside the general's mantle. But those who had acquired by his means the wealth of the exiled and murdered citizens could not risk the retribution which would follow the retirement of their protector. They pressed him to resume the generalship, and on his declaring that he would do so only without colleagues, they created him 'autocrat.'*

It now remained to deal with the exiles, who had moved from Herbita to Messana. Thither Agathocles marched, and having surprised a frontier fortress he pretended to negotiate a ransom, and meanwhile attempted to surprise Messana while off its guard. Failing in this he occupied Mylæ, and so hemmed in the town on the west. In the autumn he laid siege to it with his whole force. The Messenians begged for assistance from the Carthaginians, who sent envoys to Agathocles, bidding him withdraw and restore the captured fort on pain of war, and accusing him of breaking the peace. Being not yet prepared for so serious a war he complied, but he did not desist from his aggressions upon the other Sicilian towns. Hamilcar, the Carthaginian commander, was, indeed, in direct collusion with him, and pledged to advance him in every way as an instrument to his own designs. But as, by the Peace of Timoleon, autonomy was secured to all towns east of the Halycus, the government of Carthage could with justice accuse Agathocles of breaking the treaty. Many of these towns seem, indeed, to have placed themselves under Carthaginian protection as a defence against Agathocles.

* Justin says that Agathocles was supported in this *coup d'état* by 5,000 of Hamilcar's troops. He also says that the whole of the Six Hundred were murdered, together with many democratical leaders ; while the populace, assembled in the theatre, were there kept in check by a body of troops.

Meanwhile the exiles from Syracuse, their ranks now increased by refugees from other conquered cities, formed a coalition of Agrigentum, Gela, and Messana. Afraid to entrust one of their own number with the command— a course which seemed to result invariably in the establishment of a new *tyrannis*—they applied to Sparta for a commander. It happened that the Spartans had been defeated by Antipater, King of Macedonia, on the Peneus, in 323 B.C., and the numerous survivors of the defeat had been exempted, as in the case of Leuctra, from the ordinary ignominy visited upon such survivors. This exemption Acrotatus, son of King Cleomenes, had violently opposed, and the resentment of the survivors was so bitter as to endanger his life. He was glad, therefore, to accept the command of the confederate Sicilians, and sailed at once, calling at Tarentum *en route*, where he was joined by a fleet of twenty-eight vessels. His arrival raised high hopes, and he was soon at the head of a large force. His position turned his head. Abandoning the rigours of Spartan discipline, he paraded himself in all the luxury and self-will which the Greeks stigmatized as *Persism*. Finally, growing jealous of Sosistratus, the ex-tyrant of Syracuse and leader of the confederates, he had him assassinated at a banquet. The discontent now came to a head. He was forced to steal away to Sparta; the Tarentines, who had followed him only because he belonged to the blood-royal of their mother-city, returned home; and the members of the confederacy, at the mediation of Hamilcar, concluded peace with Agathocles.

The conduct of Hamilcar was on this occasion so manifestly philo-Syracusan that the various States under the Carthaginian protectorate made personal complaints against him at Carthage. Always ready to find a handle against a general who did them no credit, the Carthaginians could take no open action, inasmuch as Hamilcar was in possession of their Sicilian territory, and would immediately ally himself openly, in case of danger, with Agathocles. His second in command, Hamilcar, son of Gisco, was of known loyalty, but probably in no position to withstand the attack of two such powerful allies.

10

Accordingly, the Carthaginian Senate contented themselves with recalling Hamilcar Gisco, and with taking a secret ballot as concerned his superior officer, the result of which should not be disclosed until the arrival of Hamilcar Gisco in Africa. This piece of diplomacy was rendered nugatory by the death of its object, apparently about 314, 313 B.C.

Agathocles was well aware that the peace was insecure, and that Carthage would take the first occasion to set it aside. He therefore busied himself in far-sighted preparations for the coming struggle, keeping on foot a mercenary force of 10,000 men and 3,000 horse, manufacturing arms, and putting Syracuse in a state of defence. At the same time he extended his power, either by alliance or by conquest, over the various cities until he was once more checked by Messana. This town seems not to have acceded to the recent pacification, and to have become again the resort of all the Sicilian refugees. Isolated as it was, it was easily persuaded to abandon the cause of exiles who had no claim upon it. Agathocles secured the recall of such of its own citizens as had been banished for partisanship with himself, and immediately afterwards massacred 600 others who had resisted his aggressions.

With the whole of the eastern sea-board in his power, Agathocles now felt himself able to defy Carthage and to pursue his aggressions towards the west. Gela and Agrigentum, the leading cities of the late league, were now in alliance with Carthage, and thither had collected the exiles recently expelled from Messana, under Dinocrates, whom Agathocles had dismissed after the sack of Syracuse. Hamilcar was dead; and it seemed that a blow might be struck before a new general could consolidate the Carthaginian forces in Sicily. The Syracusan army was suddenly moved across the island upon Agrigentum, but found on its arrival that the Carthaginian general had already occupied the harbour with 60 vessels. Agathocles withdrew, and ravaged the Carthaginian reservation, capturing several fortresses there.

News of this insult reached Carthage at the moment when Dinocrates was present as the envoy of the exiles. Added to his representations, it spurred the Carthaginians to fresh and vigorous efforts to crush the despot before his power reached a yet greater height. Dinocrates returned with the promise of speedy and effectual help, and was greeted with the news that his general, Nymphodorus, had been cut off with an entire detachment by the Syracusans in the attempt to occupy Centoripe at the invitation of some of its inhabitants, whom Agathocles proceeded to massacre forthwith.

Meanwhile the Carthaginians, as earnest of their resolve, despatched to Sicily a fleet which sailed suddenly, unopposed, into the Great Harbour of Syracuse. It could effect little damage, however, and retired northwards, where part of it fell into the hands of Syracusan vessels off Bruttium. Dinocrates now occupied Calauria, at the invitation of its inhabitants, and being there attacked by a Syracusan army under Philonides and Pasiphilus, lieutenants of Agathocles, was defeated with loss and the road to Gela thrown open. Thither Agathocles at once marched, aware that the Carthaginians were encamped on Ecnomus, a hill in the Geloan territories. They declined battle, however, and Agathocles returned to Syracuse at the close of 312 B.C., boasting himself a match for the world.

In the year 311 B.C. Hamilcar Gisco sailed for Sicily with a fleet of 130 ships of war, 10,000 African troops, 1,000 Etruscan mercenaries, and 2,000 native Carthaginians, many of them leading citizens. He brought also 200 chariots and 1,000 Balearic slingers, and a fleet of transports laden with money, arms, and supplies of all kinds. A storm scattered the flotilla and destroyed 60 ships of war and 200 transports, while the remainder reached Sicily only with great difficulty. But Hamilcar was soon enabled to recruit his forces to the number of 40,000 foot and 5,000 horse from his Sicilian allies, whom he possessed the faculty of conciliating to a high degree. He occupied the same position as in the previous year at Ecnomus.

The kindness of Hamilcar, contrasting with the continued cruelties of Agathocles, caused widespread defection throughout the States subject to the despot—defection increased by the news that the Carthaginian fleet had swept the straits of Messana, captured a Syracusan fleet of 20 sail, and was menacing the supplies of the city itself. Gela threatened to open its gates to Hamilcar, and Agathocles determined at one blow to secure that fortress and to intimidate the wavering States. Small detachments of his troops entered the town on various pretexts, mastered it, and massacred 4,000 of the inhabitants on the charge of contemplating revolt. The remainder were stripped of all their valuables and money ; and Agathocles moved westward after securely garrisoning the place.

The Carthaginians occupied the brow of the high ground on the right bank of the Himera, where it falls into the sea 20 miles west of Gela. On the left or eastern bank was another strong position called Phalarium, and said to take its name from Phalaris, as Ecnomus from the lawlessness* of that tyrant. Here Agathocles entrenched himself ; and for one or two days the two armies faced each other, neither caring to commence the struggle, owing to superstitious dread of an oracle which declared that the spot should one day be the scene of much bloodshed. At length Agathocles, to whose interest it was to hurry on the conflict, posted an ambuscade by the river, and sent across a small body of horse to draw out the enemy by driving off their cattle and horses. His plan succeeded. The Numidian cavalry dashed down, pursued the retreating Syracusans, and found themselves entrapped in the ambuscade. They were forced to retire in their turn, and Agathocles now moved his whole force across the river to storm the opposite hill. Success seemed probable, but the services of the Balearic slingers, whose missiles weighed as much as a pound each, at length drove off the Greeks ; and when they rallied and again charged up the slope they found themselves taken in the rear by a reinforcement of

* ἐκνομία, *lawlessness.*

Carthaginian troops which had just landed at the mouth
of the Himera and moved up the valley unnoticed under
cover of the hills. Hamilcar, who had probably waited
for this to happen, now allowed his men to charge, and
the Greeks, caught between two armies, were routed with
terrible loss. Seven thousand fell, including most of the
cavalry, and Agathocles shut himself up in Gela. Without wasting time in assaulting that place, Hamilcar
moved rapidly through the island, winning over amongst
many others the numerous towns of the eastern coast,
Catana, Leontini, Tauromenium, Messana, Abacænum,
and Camarina; and Agathocles, finding his communica-
tions with Syracuse threatened, withdrew thither to
make what preparations he could to withstand the impending siege.

With all Sicily leagued against him on the side of
Hamilcar, his revenues intercepted, his cavalry and the
bulk of his mercenaries lost, with the Carthaginian fleet
blockading the harbour of Syracuse and cutting off all
supplies, Agathocles found himself reduced to extremity.
Desperation quickened his wits. With the greatest
secrecy he ordered the equipment of a fleet of 60
ships, finding funds for the purpose by stripping the
temples of their treasures, and by raising forced loans
from the wealthy merchants. The walls of Ortygia,
rebuilt upon the plan of the Dionysian fortifications,
concealed the Inner Harbour so effectually that the
whole fleet was built and manned without any rumour
of the proceeding reaching the Carthaginians. Even the
citizens were ignorant of its object, and imagined that
the despot contemplated a descent upon Italy, Sardinia,
or the Carthaginian possessions in Western Sicily. On
board was put a force levied from the flower of the remaining mercenaries, slaves armed for the purpose, and
one or more members of every Syracusan family of note.
To meet as far as possible the lack of cavalry, each horse-
man was ordered to provide himself with saddle and
bridle as harness for animals to be obtained by foray.
When all was ready Agathocles convened an assembly.
'He had hit,' he said, 'upon the one and only plan of

salvation. He would restore the failing fortunes of Syracuse; but the city itself must continue to hold the besiegers in check while he did so. All who despaired, or did not care to face the risk, were at liberty to depart.' Sixteen hundred of the leading citizens, amongst others, took advantage of this permission and prepared to quit the town, whereupon Agathocles slew them all and confiscated their property. He thus obtained additional funds, and at the same time rid himself of a large faction whose intrigues would have been dangerous. The good behaviour of the remaining citizens was secured by the presence of their relatives—brothers, sons, or parents— in the force now about to sail, where they were virtually hostages for the good conduct of those left behind. Antander, brother of the despot, with an Ætolian named Erymnon as his adviser, was left in charge of the city.

Unwilling to attempt to break out of the blockaded harbour by force, Agathocles waited some time for an opportunity to escape unattacked. At length the Cartha-·ginian squadron quitted their moorings to intercept a convoy coming up with supplies, and Agathocles at once put out to sea. The appearance of his fleet, of whose very existence they had been unaware, took the enemy completely by surprise, and while they were forming to meet the expected attack he obtained so good a start that, despite the keen pursuit which was at once made when it was found that he did not intend to fight, he was still in advance when night fell. The darkness, aided providentially by a total eclipse of the sun on the following day, enabled him to make good this advantage. For six days the chase was continued; but when the enemy at last hove in sight the fugitive fleet was already off the coast of Africa, where, after a brief engagement, Agathocles ran his vessels ashore and disembarked. Here he fortified a camp, and the Carthaginians, believing that they had driven their prey into the toils, drew off in satisfaction. But they were terribly mistaken. Agathocles had resolved on nothing less than the invasion of Africa, and he had succeeded in the first step thereto.

The total eclipse of the sun occurred on August 15,

310 B.C., which gives August 19 as the day upon which Agathocles landed in Africa. The exact spot of his debarkation is unknown; but a locality answering to the recorded name, Latomiæ (The Quarries), is situated just to the west of the Mercurian Promontory. That he was able to induce his men to push forward so strenuously upon an expedition of unknown destination, and then, when its destination was at length revealed, to fall in so readily with his plans, speaks volumes for the influence and tact of Agathocles, more particularly in face of the eclipse—a prodigy which struck terror into the hearts of his crews, as it had done previously in the case of Nicias' troops, though at the same time it saved them by frustrating the success of the enemy's pursuit.

There was much to justify a *coup de main* which was at best desperate. The maintenance of the siege at Syracuse was now a question of days, cut off as it was from all supplies of food and money; while continued reverses gave daily fresh strength to the odium against the tyrant, who might look at any moment for his overthrow by an internal rising. Even if he had been able to withstand the siege, non-success would have been as fatal to him as defeat. On the other hand, by invading Africa he hoped at least to secure the recall of Hamilcar, and so to raise the siege of Syracuse; while the mere daring of the attempt would, for awhile at least, until its issue was seen, check the disaffection of his subjects, whose hatred of the 'Barbarians' was only second to their hatred of the tyrant. Moreover, he knew Africa to be a veritable garden, teeming with plunder of the richest kind, and in no position to resist attack; he knew that the tributary cities would gladly throw off the yoke of Carthage if once they saw their way to doing so with success; he knew that the wild nomad tribes, nominally allies of Carthage, would be quick to repudiate that alliance for one which offered them a share in the plunder of the richest country of the ancient world. To remain in Syracuse was to perish by starvation or the sword. To invade Africa might possibly turn the tables entirely; at the worst, it offered a glorious revenge and a soldier's death. The spirit which animated the despot was shown by his first measures. Declaring that he had vowed the sacrifice to Ceres and Proserpine if he should but reach Africa in safety, he solemnly fired his fleet with his own hand; and the troops, which yesterday had despaired of everything, assisted with enthusiasm at the sacrifice which cut off their every hope of retreat.

Before the fears of his army could recur, Agathocles broke up his camp, and, marching southward, stormed Megalopolis,* which was, like all the Carthaginian subject-cities excepting Utica, quite unfortified. Every step of his progress increased his booty and his confidence. It was 'a land of corn, wine, and oil,' of pasturage and flocks, of luxurious villas and wealthy towns, and all absolutely undefended. Marching round the Bay of Tunis, he occupied the town of Tunes, only fourteen miles south of Carthage, and made it his base of operations.

Meantime the Carthaginian fleet, after collecting the brazen beaks of the burnt Syracusan triremes, sailed round to Carthage, where the report of Agathocles' presence in Africa, taken as proof of the destruction of the army under Hamilcar, had already spread dismay. It had even been proposed to send an embassy to Agathocles to sue for peace, when the arrival of the fleet, with its assurance of its own and Hamilcar's safety, reassured and emboldened the citizens. Hanno and Bomilcar were appointed generals, and, overlooking the perils likely to arise from the well-known rivalry of those two leaders, the Carthaginians trusted that such rivalry would serve as a mutual check upon their ambition. But the unhappy policy of punishing the general for his ill-success had not been without result. Bomilcar had no mind to risk crucifixion, and he determined to secure his personal safety by seizing the despotism. The workings of the same motives have already been seen in the case of that Hamilcar against whom the Senate passed a secret ballot.

---

* Not mentioned in any other connection than the present. Apparently a Graecised form of the common Phœnician word *magurim*, which becomes in Latin *magalia*, and in Greek usually *Megara*.

Bomilcar was his nephew, and he had therefore the additional motive of wounded honour. He led out his army with the resolve to strike, not for his country, but for himself.

The force which now took the field mustered 30,000 infantry besides chariots and cavalry, and included the entire native Carthaginian levy. To oppose it Agathocles could marshal only 13,500 men, of whom some were but half-armed; while he seems to have had as yet no cavalry worth mentioning. His right wing, confronting Bomilcar, he entrusted to his son Archagathus. He himself, with 1,000 picked men, faced the Carthaginian right wing, commanded by Hanno, and including the Sacred Band. The charge of the chariots and cavalry was apparently nullified by opening the ranks, and so allowing them to dash past with little effect. Before they could wheel and repeat their charge the whole Grecian line had advanced and was already engaged in a hand-to-hand conflict. The Carthaginian right seemed on the point of victory, when the fall of Hanno, striking panic into his men, led to their complete rout; and Bomilcar, finding himself thus left sole commander, at once attempted to draw off his men, and so leave the victory with Agathocles. His aim was to allow the invading army to break the power of Carthage, and thus open to himself the path to usurpation; for in the event of Agathocles being defeated and his army destroyed, Bomilcar would have no further excuse for retaining his office of commander; while the government would be left too strong to be attacked with any chance of success. Victory, indeed, remained with Agathocles; but Bomilcar's attempted retreat became a total flight. The camp of the Carthaginians was captured with all its stores, and 20,000 pairs of manacles intended for the conquered Greeks. Two thousand men were slain, but the loss of the victors was proportionately heavy; for the Sacred Band and the Libyans about them fought valiantly, and only fled when deserted by the rest of the line.

The first proceeding of the Carthaginians on the news of this defeat was to order a wholesale holocaust of 200 infants to Moloch as a propitiatory offering; their second, to send to Hamilcar Gisco orders to despatch an instant reinforcement to Africa.   The first measure was due to the discovery of a religious scandal, it being found that the annual sacrifices to the God had been evaded by substituting children of low birth for the noble infants prescribed as victims in the State ritual.   The second measure showed that Carthage was in a critical position, and ill able to spare troops for foreign service.   The bearers of the message to Hamilcar carried with them the beaks of Agathocles's vessels, and, suppressing all news of the defeat of Hanno and Bomilcar, Hamilcar spread the report that the armament which left Syracuse a few days before was annihilated.   He then summoned the city to instant surrender, displaying the beaks of the triremes as proof of his assertions.   But the Syracusan commanders suspected treachery.   They suppressed in their turn all that Hamilcar's envoy had announced, and at once expelled from the city 8,000 citizens who were known to be in favour of capitulation.   The refugees found shelter with Hamilcar, who now drew up his forces for the assault.   He sent, however, a second envoy, repeating his previous summons, and it was by the influence of Erymnon only that Antander, a weak-spirited man, was prevented from compliance.   The delay proved the destruction of Hamilcar's hopes, for before he could commence the assault two despatch-boats ran the blockade and brought to Ortygia the news of the complete victory of Agathocles.   Thus encouraged, the Syracusans were able to repulse the attempt to storm their walls, and Hamilcar raised the siege, despatching 5,000 men to the assistance of the government at home.

Meanwhile, Agathocles, still pushing southward, had besieged and stormed Hadrumetum and Thapsus, and had repulsed with loss an attempt to recover Tunes. His success began to bear fruit in the defection of nomad tribes in alliance with Carthage, one of which, under their chief Elymas, now openly joined him.   He next moved westward into the interior, but was recalled by the news that Elymas had rejoined the Carthaginians, and that the latter, reinforced by the troops from Sicily, were a second time assaulting Tunes. He defeated and slew Elymas, and hurrying northwards, came upon the enemy by surprise in their lines before Tunes, and routed them with the loss of 2,000 men.

The retirement of Hamilcar with his land force had in a measure relieved Syracuse, but it seems that the Carthaginian fleet had never been withdrawn, so that supplies from seaward were uncertain and scanty, while on the landward side they could only be obtained, at the risk of surprise, by foraging parties. Hamilcar himself spent some months in making a fresh circuit of the island, and about the middle of 309 B.C. again moved upon Syracuse with a force of 100,000 men. He determined, as Demosthenes did before him, to attempt the surprise of Euryalus, and with the same result. The Syracusans, suspecting his purpose, had already garrisoned that fortress with 3,400 men, who fell upon the advancing Carthaginians in the confusion born of their own numbers and the darkness, and drove them headlong over the cliffs. Hamilcar, fighting bravely, was captured alive, and as the seers had foretold him, he supped that night in Syracuse, though not in the manner in which he had anticipated. He was loaded with chains, paraded round the city, and finally killed by tortures. His head was cut off and sent to Agathocles.

The defeated army remained in its lines and the siege still continued; but the death of Hamilcar deprived it of union. The question of choosing his successor ended in a complete breach between the Grecian and Carthaginian portions of the army, and the former, amounting to a considerable section of the whole, withdrew in disgust and elected Dinocrates as their generalissimo. At this moment Agrigentum declared herself the liberator of Sicily. Dinocrates was unpopular and might easily be crushed, for his troops would desert to the banner which promised autonomy. The Carthaginians must soon leave the island to defend their home possessions. The Syracusans were too exhausted to resist anything short of actual attack. It was a brilliant opportunity of acquiring and honestly using in Sicily that position which Syracuse had usurped and abused. The Agrigentines put themselves under the command of Xenodicus, and proclaimed the freedom and independence of all Greek towns in Sicily.

These towns were, however, now mostly garrisoned by the Carthaginians. Of all the recent possessions of Agathocles only Gela and Echetla* remained to him. The former town opened its gates to Xenodicus by night, expelled the Syracusan garrison, and joined heart and soul in the cause. The storming of Echetla—a strongly fortified position occupied by a handful of Agathocles' mercenaries, who raided on the territories of Leontini and Camarina in the hope of restoring their lost ascendancy in the vicinity of Syracuse—inspired the Syracusans with fresh fear, while it encouraged the various towns to expel their garrisons and set up democratical governments. The Carthaginians, in their absorbing desire to crush Syracuse, appear to have made no effort to stay the rise of this new Grecian power in the island.

The head of Hamilcar, insolently paraded before their camp by Agathocles, showed too clearly to the Carthaginians the fate of their forces in Sicily, while it heightened the confidence of the invading army, which seems to have moved unmolested up and down the country, plundering and destroying, but never going far from the walls of Carthage. An unfortunate brawl checked this tide of success. Lyciscus, one of the most popular officers, used insulting language to his commander while intoxicated, and though Agathocles took no notice of the offence, his son Archagathus saw fit to take the law into his own hands and to assassinate the offender. The whole army at once rose in mutiny. They clamoured for revenge on the assassin, and for the arrears of pay due to them.† They chose new generals, occupied Tunes, and, putting Agathocles and his son under sur-

---

* A hill-fort commanding the overland route to Gela and Camarina, and also dominating the whole of the south-east corner of Sicily as far as Leontini.

† This curious hint shows that the booty which Agathocles obtained was less valuable than it is said to have been. The bulk of the valuables had probably been carried into Carthage by the owners; and there were none of the usual facilities for disposing advantageously of captives and plunder. Agathocles is said to have sailed from Syracuse with no more than fifty talents.

veillance, threatened to make the father's life atone for the son's misdeeds unless the latter were surrendered to punishment. At the same time they opened negotiations with the Carthaginian army close at hand, and seemed in a fair way to coming to terms. Agathocles laid aside his dress and assumed the attire of a beggar, and saying that he did not care to live if his soldiers cared not to defend him, he made a feint of committing suicide. The soldiery relented and stayed his hand. Instantly he resumed his command, put his force under arms, and, marching out, inflicted a severe defeat upon the Carthaginians, who believed that the whole Grecian army was coming up to surrender. He then hurried again into the interior in pursuit of a Carthaginian army sent to reduce the revolted Numidians. In two engagements nothing decisive was effected by either party. A body of mercenary Greeks in the service of Carthage fell into the hands of Agathocles, who put them all to death after promising to spare their lives.

At about the same time (309—308 B.C.) two additional events occurred to increase the difficulties of Carthage— the arrival of an army to reinforce Agathocles under Ophellas, King of Cyrene, and the attempt of Bomilcar to overturn the government. The city of Cyrene, now Ghrennah, was situate exactly midway between Alexandria and Carthage. Originally a colony of Spartans under Battus, it remained for many years under a dynasty of kings, called after their founder the Battiadæ; and occupying one of the few fertile spots on the coast of North Africa, it attained a high degree of prosperity.* Its territory extended westward as far as the Aræ Philæni, where it adjoined that of Carthage. When Alexander conquered Egypt, 332 B.C., Cyrene made submission to him; but on his demise, Ptolemy, son of Lagus, who succeeded to the kingdom of Egypt, seeing the city involved in an exhausting war with some exiles who were seeking to effect their return, took its part, drove the

---

* The fertility of Cyrenaica—the district round Cyrene—was proverbial. Its main product was silphium (assafœtida), the medicinal drug; whence τὸ Βάττου σιλφιον is, with Aristophanes, equivalent to an Eldorado.

exiles out of the country, and annexed the whole district. He organised it as a vice-royalty under Ophellas, late an officer in the army of Alexander, and connected by marriage with the house of the Athenian Miltiades.

The wealth of Cyrene, could it be enlisted in his service, promised materially to aid the arms of Agathocles. He invited Ophellas to bring his whole force against Carthage, promising that, in the event of success, Carthage should be the prize of Ophellas, while he himself would be content to have freed Sicily for all further fear of Carthaginian aggression. The influence of Ophellas enabled him to levy a large army—upwards of 20,000 fighting men—with which he at once struck into the Libyan desert. The march was one of terrible sufferings, beset by the dangers of thirst and snake-bites, and harassed by the incessant attacks of the Libyans. It was accomplished, however, though with heavy losses; and Agathocles found himself reinforced by an army of 10,000 Greeks, under the command of a general too powerful to be acceptable. He accused Ophellas of plotting against him, and put him to death. The Cyrenian army, left without a leader, had no choice but to throw in its fortunes with those of the assassin.

But far more dangerous to Carthage was the intestine peril which threatened her. Bomilcar, still commander-in-chief, despite his manifest treachery, on pretence of a levy, collected in the suburbs a force of 4,000 mercenaries and some 500 citizens favourable to his designs. Dividing these into five columns, he entered the city, cutting down his opponents on all sides; but the main body of the citizens, when their first alarm was over, seeing the scanty numbers of his forces, assailed him so vigorously with showers of missiles from the roofs that he was compelled to retire and fortify himself in the suburb known as Neapolis. By well-timed lenity the government induced the insurgents to lay down their arms, and dismissed them all in safety, with the exception of Bomilcar in person, whom they at once crucified. It was a fortunate thing for Carthage that Agathocles was unaware of the crisis. Had he known of it in time he might have captured the city. On the other hand, the sedition kept the Carthaginians employed when they might otherwise have taken advantage of the murder of Ophellas to draw over the whole of his army to their side.* A little later Agathocles moved round to the northern side of Carthage, and, after a short siege, took. and sacked Utica and Hippo Acra, two cities which had thus far remained loyal to Carthage. This was followed by the ravaging of the whole maritime district,† and the adhesion of many of the Numidians. Famine began to be felt in the· city, and so far superior was Agathocles now that he ventured to leave Archagathus in command, and to recross to Sicily in order to restore, if possible, something of his old ascendancy in that island. Two of his generals, Leptines and Demophilus, had recently driven Xenodicus out of the field, and at the moment when Agathocles landed at Selinus there was no force, Greek or Carthaginian, to oppose him. He re-established his authority at Heraclea Minoa, where it had only recently been disowned, and crossed to the north coast so as to avoid Agrigentum, where Xenodicus was stationed. Here he expelled the Carthaginian garrisons from Thermæ and Cephalœdium, and arrived at Syracuse in the autumn of 308 B.C., with no other reverse than the failure of an attempt upon Centoripe. His presence once more roused the entire island to arms, and, Xenodicus hanging back, Dinocrates took the command of an army of 20,000 Greeks —a force which Agathocles dared not meet in the field, but could only harass and annoy. Jealousy soon divided his opponents, and the Agrigentines placed themselves under Xenodicus. That general, compelled against his judgment to give battle to Leptines, was defeated with loss and fled to Gela. The recall of Agathocles to Africa, there to rescue the army under Archagathus, prevented his following up this success.

The removal of Bomilcar had given fresh life to the

* The chronology of these events is dubious. Justin says that there was no assault upon Carthage by Bomilcar, but that the latter was seized and executed immediately upon the discovery of his treachery, which occurred *after* a defeat of the Carthaginians by the combined armies of Agathocles and Ophellas.

† *I.e.*, the district to the north of Carthage and westward of the Bay of Tunis.

Carthaginian government. Three columns of 10,000 men each, commanded by Himilco, Adherbal, and Hanno, were despatched to act in the interior, on the coast, and in the central region respectively. Archagathus, elated by the success which had attended his lieutenant, Eumachus, in a distant expedition amongst the Numidians, made the mistake of dividing his own small force in a similar manner. In rapid succession one division, under Æschrion, was surprised and destroyed by Hanno; a second, under Eumachus, inveigled by stratagem into attacking Himilco, was defeated and compelled to surrender for lack of water; and Archagathus himself, in command of the third remaining column, found himself shut up in Tunes and there besieged by the united Carthaginian forces, now strengthened by the adhesion of all the towns which had sided with the invaders in the day of their success.

Summoned urgently to the rescue, Agathocles, reinforced by eighteen ships from Etruria, gave battle to the squadron which still blockaded Ortygia, and defeated it so completely that its admiral committed suicide to escape capture. He then joined Archagathus in Tunes. He found the troops starving and mutinous, but still numbering 12,000 Greeks and 10,000 Numidians of doubtful fidelity. With these he endeavoured to draw out the Carthaginians to battle, but the latter declined, trusting to famine to gain the victory for them. In desperation he made an assault upon the besiegers' lines, and was driven back into the town with the loss of 3,000 men. During the same night the Carthaginian camp was accidentally fired by the flames of their triumphal sacrifices and completely destroyed, while at the same time the attempted desertion of the Numidians in Agathocles' army caused a panic so disastrous that 4,000 Greeks fell by each other's hands in the confusion and darkness. This second time did chance prevent either side from profiting by the disasters of the other. Agathocles now abandoned all hope, and made a cowardly attempt to escape. Detected, he was arrested and put in chains together with his sons Archagathus and Heraclides, but was again set at liberty, on the report that the Carthaginians were advancing to assault the town, that he might organize some means of resistance. But he availed himself of the opportunity to make good his escape, deserting his whole army, and leaving even his sons in the hands of his infuriated mercenaries, who straightway put both to death in revenge for his flight, and sent immediately to treat with the besieging force. They agreed to restore all the towns still remaining in their hands for a sum of 300 talents, receiving in return permission either to take service in the Carthaginian army, or, if they preferred it, to retire to Sicily and reside at Solus. A few who still preferred to resist were captured and crucified.

It was about the end of October, 307 B.C., that Agathocles finally quitted Africa. He had maintained his position there for three years and two months, during which he had been virtually master of the entire Carthaginian possessions in Africa. But his attempt to relieve Syracuse by the diversion thus created had been only partially successful, and he seems to have in no wise repaired his exchequer by the plunder of Africa. The opportunities which continually offered themselves for making a favourable peace he declined, although he must have known how futile were his hopes of one day occupying Carthage. The only solid result of his actions was one which did not appear until long after he was dead—' he had probed the weakness of the Carthaginian empire to the very bottom, and mightier men than he . . . . were all too soon to follow in his footsteps.'* Sixty years later Regulus followed his lead with the same ill-success. More than a century later Scipio the Elder did what both Agathocles and Regulus had failed to do, and broke the power of Carthage on the field of Zama.

We do not know what had been effected by Dinocrates since the second departure of Agathocles, but the despot's return was the signal for horrors which dwarfed anything as yet achieved by him. Enraged at the failure of his attempt in Africa, and by the loss of his army there;

* *Carthage and the Carthaginians*, p. 59.

and expecting an immediate rising of all Sicily, he resolved to deter it by a deed of blood. Marching through the island, he halted before the walls of Egesta and demanded a large contribution in money. The town now numbered 10,000 inhabitants, who demurred at the magnitude of the impost. Agathocles replied by driving out and murdering all the poorer citizens in a body; the remainder he tortured to death in detail, with an inquisitorial refinement of cruelty which spared no age or sex, and did not hesitate to inflict the most horrible mutilations—a species of savagery almost unknown to the Hellenic hand. Now, too, he heard of the death of his sons in the camp at Tunes, and he took a terrible revenge. It has been said that the Syracusans who formed the original army of invasion were chosen from all the notable families of the city to serve as sureties for the good conduct of their relatives at home. These relatives were now massacred without exception by Antander at his brother's command, and numbers of families were thus cut off root and branch.

Agathocles, continuing his career of extortion, was checked by the news that his general, Pasiphilus, with the whole of the troops and towns under his command, had joined Dinocrates. Quite unmanned by this blow, he sent to Dinocrates with offers to retire altogether from Syracuse if he were allowed to retain only Thermæ and Cephalœdium. But the latter, confident in his superior numbers and aware that peace would deprive him of the command of the force by which he hoped to seize the *tyrannis* for himself, made such extravagant demands that Agathocles took fresh courage. He concluded a treaty with the Carthaginians, surrendering to them 300 talents and a large supply of corn, and all their old possessions in Sicily, and thus rid of their opposition he applied himself to dealing with Dinocrates alone. By accusing him of purposely declining the proffered peace for his own ends, he spread such disaffection amongst the ranks of his opponent's army that many of his soldiers went over to Agathocles when the latter at length ventured on an engagement near Torgium, and the whole force was destroyed either on the spot or in subsequent encounters. Dinocrates himself came to terms with the despot, and became henceforth a sort of partner in the *tyrannis* at Syracuse. It is more than probable that the victory of Agathocles at Torgium was a preconcerted affair, by which Dinocrates purchased his reward. At any rate he secured a position second only to that at which he had aimed, and he alone, of all the allies of Agathocles, never had reason to repent his alliance (306 B.C.).

From this point onwards until 264 B.C. we have nothing but fragmentary notices of Sicilian history. It seems that Agathocles, once more securely established at Syracuse, directed his arms now against Italy. He led an expedition also against the Lipari Isles, of which we have no particulars; but his main efforts seem to have been against the Bruttii, who, after forcing the Lucanians to aid them, were descending upon the Greek towns of Southern Italy. As early as 332 B.C. the latter had called in the assistance of Alexander of Epirus, who, however, was completely defeated and himself slain. In the course of the next thirty years the Romans subdued Samnium, and strengthened by their alliance, the Lucanians had become more than ever aggressive. In 307 B.C. the Tarentines called in the aid of Sparta, and King Cleonymus appeared in Italy with a large force. The close of the second Samnite war left the Tarentines isolated, and they, too, signed peace with Rome; Cleonymus sailed away and seized the island of Corcyra (304 B.C.). Within a few years the Tarentines fomented the third Samnite war (298 B.C.), and the Greek cities, again attacked by the Lucanians and Bruttians, called in the aid of Agathocles. It is probable that during his presence in Italy he came into actual collision with the Roman troops; at any rate his occupation of Crotona and Hipponium paralyzed the action of the Tarentines, and the Samnites, left to themselves, were a third time and finally reduced to peace, 290 B.C. It was during this war that Cleonymus, attacked in Corcyra by Cassander, King of Macedon, called in the aid of Agathocles, who drove off Cassander and seized the island for himself about 298 B.C. Three years later, 295 B.C., he ceded the island to Pyrrhus as a dowry with his daughter Lanassa.

In 289 B.C. he again quarrelled with the Carthaginians, and while organizing a new force to invade Africa was seized by mortal illness. He declared as his heir his son and namesake Agathocles, and directed the various garrisons to be handed over to him. One such garrison was at Ætna, commanded by a second Archagathus, son of him who had perished in Africa and grandson of the despot ; and, on the new ruler appearing to take over the troops, Archagathus assassinated him. The dying tyrant, having nothing to hope for from the lenity of his grandson, despatched to Egypt, to the protection of Ptolemy, his wife Theoxena and his remaining children. He died shortly after, and dying heard that the Carthaginians had once more overrun the greater part of the island, which had owed what little immunity from barbarian encroachment it ever enjoyed only to the still greater barbarism of its Greek tyrant.

Agathocles presents even more truly than Dionysius the Elder the ideal of outrageous *tyrannis*. A self-seeker from the first, he had attained the despotism by means which even Dionysius did not employ—the sack and pillage of the city he wished to rule. Like Dionysius he had spent the whole of his life in war, and each despot had brought ruin and misery upon Sicily at large—the latter in greater measure than the former. But there was in Agathocles none of the patronage of literature or the architectural munificence which made the Syracuse of Dionysius the leading city of Hellas, and cruel as Dionysius undoubtedly was, his character appears mild and forgiving by the side of the brutal temper of Agathocles

CHAPTER XII.

Literature.

Small remains of purely Sicilian Literature—The Native School of Comedians—Epicharmus, Phormis, and Dinolochus—The Mimes of Sophron — Stesichorus, Pindar, Simonides, Bacchylides — The Transition—Sicilian Rhetoric—Corax, Tisias, and Gorgias—Empedocles—The *Birds* of Aristophanes—The Second Period; Court of Dionysius the Elder—The Poets—Philoxenus and Dionysius—The Historians—Philistus—Decay of Literature in the time of Dionysius II.—Timæus—the Later Comedians—Theocritus—The Authorities for this History—Diodorus Siculus—Justinus.

THE wealth of Sicily, fostering the brilliant Hellenic genius, gave birth to numbers of poets, historians, and orators between the years 500 and 290 B.C., yet of all that number one only has survived in anything but the barest fragments, and most of them are names and nothing more. The old Dorian vintage songs developed into a perfect form of comedy, the brief space of freedom in the middle of the fifth century B.C. produced a brilliant school of rhetoricians, before the Attic comedy had obtained recognition, and while oratory was still a gift, not an art, in the foremost state of Greece. Towards the end of the fourth century B.C. was born Theocritus, whose poems have remained for all time the type of pastoral poetry—a poetry which had no counterpart at all in Attica. His works alone survive of all that was written in these three peculiarly Sicilian branches of literature by native Sicilians.*

Sicily gained, however, an especial fame as the patron

---

* The poems of Bion and Moschus, imitators of Theocritus, also survive in part; but the former (flourished 280 B.C.) was a native of Smyrna, and both come later than the period under notice. Moschus flourished 250 B.C.

of all the litterateurs of Hellas, under the rule of the earlier tyrants. The double-sided education of the Greek left its stamp upon the man, whether a citizen in a free democracy or despot of a subject people. The tyrants exercised their power mainly by the aid of physical strength ; but there always remained the national desire to excel in 'music' also—the accomplishments of the mind. Hence came the splendid theories of the despots to Olympia, Nemea, Delphi, and the Isthmus ; hence the peaceful triumphs of Thero, Gelo, and Hiero with their chariots, and of Dionysius with his tragedies ; and hence came that patronage of literature—more particularly poetry—for which the courts of Gelonian and Dionysian dynasts were famous, and which was the one possible saving feature in the character of the sternest of despots. The literature of the fifth and fourth centuries of Sicily divides naturally into two periods of brilliancy followed by two periods of transition, less known but not therefore less prolific. The two eras of florescence are those of the Gelonian despotism, 485—470 B.C., and of the *tyrannis* of the Elder Dionysius, 400—367 B.C.

The Sicilian Comedy, which attained perfection about a generation earlier than the Old Comedy of Athens, was developed spontaneously in Sicily. In character it was something between the Old Comedy of Aristophanes and the Comedy of Criticism to which the latter gave place. It consisted largely of mythological travesties, not unlike the later Satyric Drama of Athens, and contained at the same time sufficient of the political element to afford possibly a pattern for the Aristophanic Comedy. This is, however, doubtful. The political allusions in Sicilian Comedy must necessarily have been mild and guarded under the surveillance of a Gelo or Hiero, and it does not seem that this branch of the drama retained its characteristics later than the close of the Gelonian supremacy. More peculiar to it were the semi-philosophical and critical discourses with which it abounded, which were at once the prototype of the Athenian Comedy of Criticism (after 410 B.C.) and of the sententious dialogues of the

Athenian Tragedy whose first master, Æschylus, must have imbibed their style during his sojourn in Sicily.

Epicharmus, the father of Sicilian Comedy according to Plato, was a native of Cos who migrated early to Megara in Sicily and was removed thence to Syracuse by Gelo. He is said to have been, like most Coans, a skilful physician, and he had considerable influence in the Court of Hiero. He died before 440 B.C. The 'Menæchmi' of Plautus is said to have been modelled upon a play of Epicharmus.

The names of two other comedians of this school remain, Phormis and Dinolochus. The former was tutor to the sons of Gelo; the latter is said to have been the son of Epicharmus, and a native of either Syracuse or Agrigentum. He flourished about 480 B.C. Phormis is possibly the same as Phormus the Mænalian who served in the armies of both Gelo and Hiero with distinction. In this case he was by birth an Arcadian. He is said to have introduced the use of purple skins as a covering for the stage.

Sophron, son of Agathocles and a native of Syracuse, introduced his famous Mimes at about the time of the fall of the Gelonian dynasty. These were dialogues for all kinds of characters, written like the Comedies of Epicharmus in the Doric dialect, the prevailing dialect of the Sicilian Greeks. Whether they were in prose or verse is doubtful; Professor Mahaffy suggests that they may have been of a similar style to the poems of the American writer, Walt Whitman. They took their names from low-life and were certainly coarse; but they were marked by a dramatic power and vigour which rapidly made them popular, and Plato is said to have studied them as the best model for his own philosophical dialogues. Sophron left a son, Xenarchus, who was sufficiently successful in the same line of genius to be hired by Dionysius I. when that tyrant wished to have the Rhegines lampooned on the stage of Syracuse.

The tragedian Æschylus may be mentioned here as having resided in Sicily for some years. He is said to have left Athens in 468 B.C., disgusted with the success of the young Sophocles, who obtained the first prize at the great Dionysia of that year. He resided chiefly in Sicily until his death, which occurred at Gela, 456 B.C. The first year of his Sicilian life was spent in the court of Hiero.

But the Gelonian era of literature derives its main lustre chiefly from the visits of three great lyric poets, Pindar, Simonides, and Bacchylides, who spent many years of their life at the courts of Gelo and Hiero. The Greek lyrists of the previous age had found their patrons in the courts of the tyrants of Corinth, Athens, Samos, and elsewhere. They now followed the transfer of the area of despotism to Sicily. The despot paid munificently for the panegyrics (*encomia*) which extolled his praises, the dirges (*threni*) which mourned his grief, the epitaphs which commemorated the dead; for the processional and choric songs (*prosodia* and *hyporchemata*) which were sung at his festivals and feasts; for hymns to the Gods, dithyrambs, pæans, odes to his successes in the games (*epinicia*), and drinking songs (*paræmia*). These were the special study of the lyric poets, and hence their great favour in the tyrant's eyes.

Long before the days of Pindar had flourished Stesichorus of Himera, the earliest of Sicilian poets. With Alcman he shared the honour of the headship of Dorian poetry, and he was the first of the poets to break away from the old division between the lyric and epic styles, and to adapt the subjects of the latter to the music of the former. Though his efforts never reached the perfection of the Pindaric odes, yet they approximated very nearly to them; and he is generally regarded as the pioneer of the great Gelonian lyrists. He died as early as 552 B.C., having been a contemporary of Phalaris in Sicily, and of Pittacus, Alcæus, and Sappho in Eastern Hellas. Ibycus of Rhegium, a court poet of Polycrates, despot of Samos, followed in the steps of Stesichorus, but did not live long enough to improve upon him, and his fame rests mostly on the pretty story of the ' Cranes of Ibycus,' who betrayed his murderers in the Theatre of Corinth.

Pindar (522—442 B.C.) was a native of Bœotia, where he chiefly resided; but the world-wide fame which he early acquired rendered him the envied guest of all the Hellenic courts—at Cyrene, in Macedonia, at Agrigentum, where he visited Thero, and at Syracuse, where Hiero entertained him for four years (473—469 B.C.). His surviving poems are all *Epinicia*—songs commemorating the victories of winners at the four great Hellenic festivals, to each of which one book is devoted. Amongst these winners are Thero, Gelo, Hiero, and Psaumis of Camarina.

Simonides (556—467 B.C.) was a native of Ceos. He lived at Athens at the court of the despot Hipparchus, next amongst the despot-oligarchies of Thessaly, and again at Athens, where he carried off no less than fifty-six prizes, conquered Æschylus in a competition for an elegy on those who fell at Marathon, and finally went to Syracuse (476 B.C.), where he lived until his death. He was the great poet of elegy, mournful lyrics in alternate hexameter and pentameter lines, and he rivalled Pindar in the composition of odes. The latter poet's jealousy leads him to make continual innuendoes as to the avarice of his rival, whom he declares to have been the first to prostitute the art of poetry by taking money for his works. Numerous epitaphs by Simonides remain—notably that on the Spartans who were killed at Thermopylæ—and a large number of fragments. He is to be distinguished carefully from his namesake, the iambic poet of Amorgos, who lived about 660 B.C.

Of Bacchylides, nephew of Simonides of Ceos, there remain only two epigrams and a number of fragments. He flourished about 475 B.C., and lived long at the Syracusan court, composing pæans, odes, and dithyrambs.

With the expulsion of Thrasybulus and the Liberation disappeared most of the munificence which had maintained the brilliant lyricists of the previous era. These were still employed to celebrate the victories at the great festivals, but they no longer had any fixed Hellenic court to which they could congregate. In Sicily the Liberation brought with it the famous rhetorical school. Rhetoric

—the art of oratory—could find no play under the rule
of despots, who suppressed all public debate. With the
sudden growth of democracy came the attendant art of
swaying popular assemblies. It never attained in Sicily
the logical and scientific accuracy and method which
characterized the rhetoric of the Athenians of the fourth
century B.C., being stamped out while still in its infancy
by the despotism of the Dionysii. It was distinguished
rather by the features natural to an art as yet empirical
and untrained—by the lavish use of mere figures of speech
and ornamental language, metaphor, and excessive tendency towards striking and often false antitheses. Nevertheless, its first utterances from the lips of Gorgias in the
Athenian Assembly produced a great effect, and led to the
immediate study of rhetoric in that State.

Corax, of Syracuse, was the pioneer of Sicilian rhetoric. So powerful was his oratory that he became
the leading figure in the State upon the expulsion of
Thrasybulus. He composed the earliest treatise on
rhetoric, which he called simply ' The Art ' *(Techne)*, and
his work long retained its value with later rhetoricians.
Contemporary with him was Tisias, of whom nothing is
known beyond that he taught at Thurii, where Lysias
was one of his pupils.

But the greatest of the Sicilian rhetors was Gorgias of
Leontini (born 480 B.C.). In the year 427 B.C. he conducted the embassy which applied to Athens for help
against the Sicilian Dorians, and made so great an impression that many Athenians at once became his pupils,
amongst them Alcibiades, Antisthenes, and Æschines.
He was a master of effective alliteration and antithesis,
and prided himself on the nice balance of his periods.
Besides being a rhetorician, he was also a sophist and
philosopher. He wrote epideictic speeches, or declama-
tions intended only for display, and there remain two
of doubtful authenticity, the ' Apology of Palamedes,' and
the ' Encomium of Helen.' He spent the later years of
his life, after 420 B.C., in Greece and Thessaly, dying at
the age of over a hundred years. In the dialogue entitled *Gorgias*, Plato represents him as arguing on the

value of rhetoric with Socrates and others. Polus, of Agrigentum, a disciple of Gorgias, wrote several works. He appears as one of the characters in the Platonic dialogue just mentioned.

Lysias, the Attic orator, need be mentioned only as a pupil of Tisias, at Thurii. His Sicilian training shows itself but slightly in his speeches, which are the very model of Attic oratory. To his harangue was due the insult offered by the Greeks to the Theory of Dionysius I. at Olympia, 384 B.C. Amongst the other Attic orators Isocrates shows very clearly the study of Sicilian models.

Mention has already been made* of the schools of Pythagoras and Parmenides, which flourished so extensively throughout Western Hellas at this period. The only native Sicilian philosopher of whom any writings remain was Empedocles, of Agrigentum, who flourished about 444 B.C., and was the teacher of Gorgias. He was one of the leading actors in the revolution which expelled Thrasydæus, and in the later overthrow of The Thousand. His philosophy dealt mainly with natural phenomena, and he therefore ranked amongst the early physiologists. He is said to have prevented the malaria which prevailed at Agrigentum by his schemes of drainage, and to have been so successful a physician as to win the name of a magician—a reputation which he studied to maintain. He even threw himself into the crater of Ætna, that the mystery of his disappearance might never be solved, and that it might be attributed to a deathless apotheosis. He wrote, amongst other works, all in poetry, a book explaining his system of natural philosophy (περὶ φύσεως), and a poem entitled ' Purifications' (καθαρμοί), recommending virtuous living as a means of avoiding maladies. Lucretius thought highly of him, and made him his model in the poem *De Rerum Natura*.

The years succeeding Gorgias' retirement from Sicily have left no literature of Sicilian origin until the era of Dionysius I. Nevertheless, the Sicilian expedition influenced the literature of Athens considerably, and one

* See page 114.

example of this is probably left in the *Birds* of Aristophanes, which seems to ridicule the inordinate ambition
and hopes of the Athenians for empire in Sicily, which is
represented by Nephelococcygia—'Cuckoo-town in the
Clouds.' The sixth and seventh books of Thucydides'
history are almost entirely devoted to the details of the
Sicilian expedition, and it is not unlikely that the author,
who became an exile in 423 B.C., visited Syracuse. His
predecessor, Herodotus, certainly migrated to Thurii,
where he died.

With the firm establishment of Dionysius began the
second era of Sicilian literature; but it was now rather
an era of prose writers than of poets, although Philoxenus
was a poet of considerable ability, and Dionysius himself,
as has been said, competed successfully for the prize of
Tragedy. Philoxenus (435—380) was a native of Cythera,
who was sold in his youth as a slave, and resided for
some years at Athens, where the poet Melanippides in-
structed him in dithyrambic poetry. He migrated afterwards to Syracuse, where he was long in high favour.
He fell into disgrace, however, for the severe criticisms
which he passed on the verses of Dionysius, and was imprisoned. Soon released, he never quite regained his
position, and ultimately went to Ephesus, where he died,
380 B.C. He wrote, amongst other poems, a dithyrambic
ode entitled *Cyclops* (or *Galatea),* and another named
The Banquet ($\Delta\varepsilon\tilde{\iota}\pi\nu o\nu$), describing the luxurious living of
the despot. Only fragments remain of either work.

Of the compositions of Dionysius nothing is known but
the title of the play—'The Ransom of Hector'—which
conquered at the Athenian Lenæa of 367 B.C., and so led
indirectly to its author's illness and death.

The chief writer of prose was Philistus, a native of
Syracuse, who assisted Dionysius I. in his usurpation, and
was for many years his leading minister. He was then
banished, and retired to Adria, where he composed his
history. He returned on the accession of Dionysius II.,
and remained the chief adviser of that tyrant when he
had secured the banishment of his rival Dion. His death

has already been described.* His history consisted of two parts. The former, comprising seven books, recounted the history of Sicily down to the sack of Agrigentum, 406 B.C.; the second related the history of Dionysius I. in four books, and that of Dionysius II. in two more. Only a few fragments remain. His style was modelled closely on that of Thucydides.

There must have been many other authors at the court of Syracuse at this period, for it rivalled the literary brilliancy of the days of the Gelonian dynasty. None, however, have survived; and the troubles which followed the death of Dionysius the Elder soon broke up the circle which had gathered about him, particularly when his successor quarrelled with Dion and threw off his brief enthusiasm for intellectual pursuits. The years between 367—339 B.C. were years of misery, in which no such pursuits could thrive, and with Plato literature virtually quitted Sicily until the time of Timoleon and the Second Liberation. The succeeding years produced more fruit as peace and security returned; but even in the worst of the years of oppression a few glimpses of better things may be seen. The tyrant Mamercus was an author of tragedies of no mean merit; Athanis wrote history; Archytas and his followers studied philosophy in Magna Græcia, as did Æschines at Syracuse, himself a disciple of Socrates. Of the relationship of Plato's philosophy to this period full details have been given already.†

The town of Tauromenium, which was the first to welcome Timoleon, was the birthplace of Timæus the historian, whose father Andromachus was the leading citizen of that town. He was born about 350 B.C.; but of his life nothing is known, save that he was banished by Agathocles, and died at the age of ninety-six at Athens, where he had resided for fifty years. He was the author of a voluminous History of Sicily from the earliest times down to 264 B.C., when Philinus and Polybius took up the thread of his narrative. The work exceeded forty books, and though Polybius often attacks it, it had the merit of being full of archæological details, of which the

---

* See page 121.   † See page 113 sqq.

loss is irreparable. He was the first writer to introduce the system of chronology which dates events by Olympiads. Only fragments remain.

During the years of the Liberation there was a revival of the dramatic art in Sicily. Sosicles of Syracuse, who flourished 340—320 B.C., wrote seventy-three tragedies, and was seven times a victor. Nothing is known of his plays, and he seems to have been almost isolated in his pursuit of the tragic drama. The names of comedians are a little more numerous. Chief amongst them were Philemon and Apollodorus. The former was a native of Soli or Syracuse; he probably resided at the latter place for some time. He began to exhibit in 330 B.C., and was considered by some even superior to Menander, the greatest writer of the Comedy of Manners. Even Quinctilian, the critic, places him second. He imitated the style of Euripides, and of the fifty-three comedies of which the names survive, The Treasure ($\theta\eta\sigma\alpha\upsilon\varrho\delta\varsigma$) was translated by Plautus as the *Trinummus*. Apollodorus of Gela was another contemporary of Menander (whose date is 342—291 B.C.). The *Phormio* of Terence was a translation of a play of his, as was also Terence's *Hecyra* according to one account, though another attributes it to Menander in its original form. This Apollodorus was confounded with a namesake, a native of Carystus, who ranked as one of the six masters of the New Comedy.

About the time of Sosicles flourished Alexis of Thurii, the uncle and teacher of Menander, and author of no less than two hundred and forty-five comedies.

The poet Theocritus belongs strictly to the middle of the third century B.C., but something may be said of him here. The date of his birth is unknown. He was a Syracusan, son of Praxagoras and Philinna, and early removed to Alexandria, afterwards returning to Sicily, where he lived at the court of Hiero II. in the time of the first Punic War. The *Idylls* which go by his name are not all genuine, and the same applies to the twenty-two epigrams and the fragments of a poem called *Berenice* which are attributed to him. He was the first writer of Bucolic, or Pastoral Poetry, but some of his genuine

Idylls are *encomia* on Hiero and on Ptolemy Soter, King of Egypt, who patronized the poet when at Alexandria. The purely bucolic idylls describe the everyday life of the Sicilian peasantry without any of that false simplicity and virtue which characterizes later bucolic poetry. He found imitators in Bion and Moschus, in Vergil, whose Eclogues are freely copied from the idylls, and in every later age down to the Corydons and Phyllides of the English poets of the eighteenth century. His is the last great name in Sicilian literature, the most individual, and at the same time the only name which possesses a reality for modern thought. All the others are little more than shadows, since their writings have in every case all but perished. And hence the gaps which occur in our knowledge of the history of even Syracuse, and the almost total blank in our knowledge of other Sicilian States. Nothing can repair the loss of the histories of Philistus and Timæus. Our sole authorities for any continuous history are Diodorus Siculus, a native of Agyrium, and contemporary with Cæsar and Augustus, and Justinus. But the work of the former, aiming at being a univeral history, naturally allows of little detail except in the case of such events as those of the lives of Dionysius and Agathocles, and even these are interrupted by the loss of portions. Of the forty books only fifteen survive in a complete form, including the history of the known world from 480 to 302 B.C. Justinus (a writer whose date is unknown, but probably about the third or fourth century A.D.) has left merely a digest of the forty-four books of the 'Historiæ Philippicæ' of Pompeius Trogus, and is as brief as epitomizers usually are, or even more so. These scanty materials are eked out by the help of casual notices in Herodotus for the period prior to 480 B.C.; by the sixth and seventh, and portions of other books of Thucydides; by Plutarch's Lives of Dion, Timoleon, and Nicias, and incidental allusions in other Lives; by the fragments of the historians of Sicily; and by those of Ephorus of Cymæ, who wrote a Universal History down to the year 341 B.C., in thirty books, largely utilized by Diodorus. These, and still slighter allusions and hints in the writings of Greek and Roman poets, orators, and historians, constitute the entire stock of materials for the history of one of the most famous islands in the world—an island whose soil was the scen of some of the greatest struggles and triumphs of the Greeks, and the seat of some of their noblest cities.

February, 1890.

Catalogue of Books

FOR THE EXAMINATIONS OF THE

UNIVERSITY OF LONDON.

LONDON: W. B. CLIVE & CO.,

UNIV. CORR. COLL. PRESS WAREHOUSE,

13 BOOKSELLERS ROW, STRAND, W.C.

University Correspondence College.

LONDON OFFICE : 12½ BOOKSELLERS ROW, STRAND, W.C.

FREE GUIDES TO

LONDON UNIVERSITY EXAMS.

MATRICULATION GUIDE.—No. VII., January, 1890.

CONTENTS : Hints—Regulations—Advice on Text-Books suitable for Private Students (including the Special Subjects)—The Examination Papers set Jan., 1890.

INTERMEDIATE ARTS GUIDE.—No. IV., July, 1889.

CONTENTS : Hints—Regulations—Advice on Text-Books suitable for Private Students (including the Special Subjects)—The Examination Papers set July, 1889.

B.A. GUIDE.—No. III., October, 1889.

CONTENTS : Hints (including advice on the choice of optional subjects)—Regulations— Advice on Text-Books suitable for Private Students (including the Special Subjects)—The Examination Papers set October, 1889, printed in full.

A Copy of the "**Matriculation Guide**" *may be obtained by any Private Student who expresses his intention of working for the Examination, the* "**Inter. Arts Guide**" *by any Private Student who gives date of Matriculation, and the* "**B.A. Guide**" *by any Private Student who gives date of passing Inter. Arts,* **free on application** *to the*—

SECRETARY, 12½ **Booksellers Row, London, W.C.**

Univ. Corr. Coll. Tutorial Series.

The Tutorial Series consists of Text-Books and Guides specially written to meet the requirements of the various London University Examinations by Tutors of UNIVERSITY CORRESPONDENCE COLLEGE.

All Latin and Greek Classics prescribed for London University are translated in the *Tutorial Series,* and also edited if no thoroughly suitable commentary has already been issued. Vocabularies in order of the Text are prepared for Matriculation and Intermediate Arts.

The expense involved in purchasing, for the study of short periods of History and Literature, a large book which often contains a few pages only of relevant matter is obviated by the issue of works specially written for the purposes of the Examination. Such works are provided in the *Tutorial Series* for each Intermediate Arts Examination, and also for B.A. whenever there is a distinct want.

In fine, the *Tutorial Series* fills the gap which students seeking editions of the special subjects prescribed by London University will find existing in current literature.

Among the contributors to this series are the following graduates:—

A. J. WYATT, M.A. Lond., First of his year in Branch IV. (English and French), Teachers' Diploma, Early English Text Society's Prizeman.

B. J. HAYES, M.A. Lond., First in First-Class Honours in Classics both at Inter. and B.A., Gold Medallist in Classics at M.A.

W. F. MASOM, B.A. Lond., First-Class Honours (Classics) at B.A., Double Honours (French and English) at Inter. Arts, Second in Honours at Matric., University Exhibitioner.

M. T. QUINN, M.A. Lond., First of his year in Branch I.; First in First Class Honours in Classics both at Inter. Arts and B.A., Professor at Pachaiyappa's College, Madras; late Tutor of University Correspondence College.

S. MOSES, M.A. Oxon. (Double Hons.) and B.A. Lond., First in Honours at Matriculation, Exhibitioner in Latin at Inter. Arts, and First Class Classical Honourman at B.A.

G. F. H. SYKES, B.A. Lond., Classical Honours, Assistant Examiner at London University.

A. H. ALLCROFT, B.A. Oxon., First Class Honours at Moderations and at Final Classical Exam.

C. S. FEARENSIDE, B.A. Oxon., Honours in Modern History and Classics (First Class).

W. H. LOW, M.A. Lond. (German and English).

J. WELTON, M.A. Lond., First of his year in Mental and Moral Science, bracketed equal as First of the B.A.'s at Degree Exam., Honours in French at B.A. and in English at Inter.

G. H. BRYAN, M.A., Fifth Wrangler, First Class, First Division, in Part II., Fellow of St. Peter's College, Cambridge.

R. W. STEWART, B.Sc. Lond., First in First Class Honours in Chemistry at Inter. Sc., and First in First Class Honours in Physics at B.Sc.

The Tutorial Series.—Matriculation.

MATRICULATION DIRECTORY, with **FULL AN-SWERS** to the Examination Papers. No. VII., Jan., 1890. **1s.** Cloth gilt, **1s. 6d.**

CONTENTS: Introductory Hints—University Regulations—Advice on the choice of Text-Books (including Special Subjects)—Matriculation Examination Papers set Jan., 1890—**Full Solutions** to all the above **Examination Papers** by the following Tutors of University Correspondence College:—

B. J. HAYES, M.A. Lond., First in First Class Honours in Classics at Inter. and B.A., Gold Medallist in Classics at M.A.

W. F. MASOM, B.A. Lond., First Class Honours in Classics at B.A., French and English Honours at Inter., 2nd in Honours at Matric., &c.

A. J. WYATT, M.A. Lond., Head of the M.A. List in English and French, Teachers' Diploma, &c.

L. J. LHUISSIER, B.A. Lond., First in Honours at Inter. and Final, B.-ès-Sc., B.-ès-L. Paris, also of Stuttgart and Strasburg Universities.

W. H. LOW, M.A. Lond. (German and English).

G. H. BRYAN, M.A., Fifth Wrangler, First Class, First Div. in Part II., Smith's Prizeman, Fellow of St. Peter's College, Cambridge.

C. W. C. BARLOW, M.A., Sixth Wrangler, First Class in Part II. of Math. Tripos, Mathematical Honourman at Inter. Arts, Lond.

W. H. THOMAS, B.Sc. Lond., First in First Class Honours in Chemistry.

R. W. STEWART, B.Sc. Lond., First in First Class Honours in Chemistry at Inter. Sc., and First in First Class Honours in Physics at B.Sc.

H. E. SCHMITZ, B.Sc. Lond., Neil Arnott Exhibitioner, University Scholar in Physics.

"Books, method of study, and other matter of importance are treated with a fulness of knowledge that only experts can possess."—*Educational News.*

"Practically indispensable."—*Private Schoolmaster.*

Matriculation Directory. Nos. I., II., III. (containing the Exam. Papers of Jan. and June, 1887, and Jan., 1888; with ANSWERS to the Mathematical Questions), **6d.** each. Nos. IV., V., VI. (containing the Exam. Papers of June, 1888, and Jan. and June, 1889, with **full Answers**), **1s.** each.

Matriculation Exam. Papers (in all subjects). June, 1889, and Jan., 1890, **3d.** each set.

*** To facilitate the use of these Questions at school examinations, each Paper has been printed on a leaf by itself, and may easily be torn out without injury to the rest of the book.

The Tutorial Series—Matriculation.

Matriculation Latin. By B. J. HAYES, M.A. Lond. Second Edition, Enlarged. **1s. 6d.**

CONTENTS: Choice of Text-Books—Plan of Study for 18 Weeks, with Notes and Hints—Matric. Exam. Papers in Latin Grammar from 1881 to 1889—Illustrative Sentences for Latin Prose—List of words differing in meaning according to quantity—Model Solutions, &c.

"The introductory advice to the student is very practical, and in every way admirable."—*School Board Chronicle*.

"It needs only to be seen to be thoroughly appreciated by any candidate for the Matric. Exam., and if the plan of work laid down be carried out, there cannot be a failure."—*Private Schoolmaster*.

London Undergraduate Unseens: A Reprint of all the Latin and Greek Passages set for Unprepared Translation at Matriculation and Intermediate Arts, together with schemes for reading in order of difficulty. **1s. 6d.**

Latin Syntax and Composition. By A. H. ALLCROFT, B.A. Oxon., and J. H. HAYDON, M.A. Camb. & Lond. **1s. 6d.** KEY, **2s. 6d.**
[*Ready shortly.*

Matriculation French Papers: A Reprint of the last Twenty-two Examination Papers in French set at Matriculation; with Model Answers to the Paper of June, 1888, by W. F. MASOM, B.A. Lond. **1s.**; cloth gilt, **1s. 6d.**

Matriculation English Language Papers. A Reprint of the last Twenty-two Examination Papers; with Model Answers to the Paper of June, 1889, by A. J. WYATT, M.A. Lond., and W. F. MASOM, B.A. Lond. **1s.**; cloth gilt, **1s. 6d.**

Matriculation English History Papers. A Reprint of the last Thirty-two Examination Papers; with Model Answers to that of June, 1888, by W. F. MASOM, B.A. Lond. **1s.** cloth gilt, **1s. 6d.**

** *To facilitate the use of these Questions at school examinations, each Paper has been printed on a leaf by itself, and may easily be torn out without injury to the rest of the book.*

Matriculation Mathematics. By a Cambridge Wrangler and a Mathematical Scholar. Third Edition. **1s. 6d.**

CONTENTS: Hints—Choice of Text-Books—Scheme of Study for 18 Weeks—18 Test-Papers—66 Miscellaneous Questions—256 Selected Examples—Answers—Model Solutions to 5 Sets of Examination Papers—List of Euclid's Propositions set at Matriculation during 10 years.

"Here we have a book which will save the candidate for Matriculation many an hour's profitless grind and doubtful groping. . . . The Cambridge Wrangler and Mathematical Scholar (who are also London University men) who have written it have had a wide experience in the requirements of Matriculation candidates, and know the specialities of the Examination."—*Educational Journal*.

"A great boon to private students, since a careful use of it will save them time and trouble."—*Private Schoolmaster*.

"Will no doubt serve its purpose excellently."—*Journal of Education*.

6

PUBLISHED BY W. B. CLIVE & CO.. BOOKSELLERS ROW, STRAND.

The Tutorial Series—Matriculation.

Text-Book of Heat and Light, embracing the entire Matriculation Syllabus, with an Appendix containing the three Papers set since the change in the Regulations, full Answers, and a selection of the more difficult Questions set during the last 20 years under the old regulations. By R. W. STEWART, B.Sc. Lond. **3s. 6d.**

Text-Book of Magnetism and Electricity, embracing the entire Matriculation Syllabus, with an Appendix containing the three Papers set since the change in the Regulations, full Answers and a selection of Questions set at Inter. Sc. suitable for Matriculation. By R. W. STEWART, B.Sc. Lond. **3s. 6d.**

[*In preparation.*

Matriculation Chemistry. NOTES and PAPERS. Second Edition Enlarged. **1s. 6d.**

CONTENTS: Advice on Text-Books—Definitions and Theory—Notes for 16 Lessons—18 Test Papers—Answers and Model Solutions—Glossary.

Matriculation Mechanics Papers. The last Twenty-six PAPERS set at London Matriculation, with Solutions to June, 1888, and Jan. and June, 1889, Hints on Text-Books, and 199 Additional Questions, with Results. **1s.** ; cloth gilt, **1s. 6d.**

Introduction to Inter. Arts Greek. [*In preparation.*

A Synopsis of Constitutional History. By W. F. MASOM. B.A. Lond. [*Ready shortly.*

OPINIONS OF THE PRESS ON THE TUTORIAL SERIES.

" *The Tutorial Series* (published at the London Warehouse of University Correspondence College, a new but useful and thriving adjunct to the ordinary educational machinery) is the best of its kind."—*Educational Times.*

" The University Correspondence College Tutorial Guides to the London University Examinations have gained a great reputation, just as the Correspondence College has earned a high distinction among students." — *School Board Chronicle.*

" In the way of Guides to the Examinations of the London University, the University Correspondence College Tutorial Series seems to have developed a speciality, and so far as we can see has outstripped all its rivals."—*Practical Teacher.*

" This series of Guides to the Examinations of London University will prove extremely serviceable to candidates. They give just the kind of direction and advice that a student needs, pointing out the most reliable, helpful, and recent sources of information, and plainly indicating points of special importance. Drawn up in a useful and workmanlike fashion, the books give abundant proof of sound scholarship specialised and applied to the requirements of the London examinations."—*Schoolmaster.*

" These books save the students an immense labour, and, being from the pens of professional scholars, the information is not only correctly stated, but easily understood."—*Educational Journal.*

The Tutorial Series—Matriculation.

SPECIAL SUBJECTS.

FOR JANUARY, 1890.

Ovid, Metamorphoses, Book XI. Edited by a First Class Honours Graduate of Oxford and London.

> PART I.: TEXT, INTRODUCTION, and NOTES. **1s. 6d.**
> PART II.: VOCABULARIES in order of the Text, with TEST PAPERS. **6d.** *Interleaved*, **9d.**
> PART III.: A LITERAL TRANSLATION. **1s.**
> THE THREE PARTS COMPLETE. **2s. 6d.**

"Most excellent notes, occupying three times as many pages as are occupied by the poet's lines."—*School Board Chronicle.*

Ovid, Tristia, Book III. By the Editor of Ovid's *Metamorphoses, XI.*

> PART I.: TEXT, INTRODUCTION, and NOTES. **1s. 6d.**
> PART II.: VOCABULARIES in order of the Text, with TEST PAPERS. **6d.** *Interleaved,* **9d.**
> PART III.: A LITERAL TRANSLATION. **1s.**
> THE THREE PARTS COMPLETE. **2s. 6d.**

FOR JUNE, 1890.

Cicero, De Amicitia. Edited by S. MOSES, M.A. Oxon. and B.A. Lond., and G. F. H. SYKES, B.A. Lond.

> PART I.: TEXT, INTRODUCTION, and NOTES. **1s. 6d.**
> PART II.: A VOCABULARY (in order of the Text), with TEST PAPERS. *Interleaved*, **1s.**
> PART III.: A LITERAL TRANSLATION. **1s.**
> THE THREE PARTS COMPLETE. **2s. 6d.**

Cicero, Pro Balbo. Edited by S. MOSES, M.A. Oxon. and B.A. Lond., and G. F. H. SYKES, B.A. Lond.

> PART I.: TEXT, INTRODUCTION, and NOTES. **1s. 6d.**
> PART II.: A VOCABULARY (in order of the Text), with TEST PAPERS. *Interleaved*, **1s.**
> PART III.: A LITERAL TRANSLATION. **1s.**
> THE THREE PARTS COMPLETE. **2s. 6d.**

The Tutorial Series—Matriculation.

SPECIAL SUBJECTS.

FOR JANUARY, 1891.

Horace, Odes, Book I. Edited by A. H. ALLCROFT, B.A. Oxon., and B. J. HAYES, M.A. Lond.

> PART I.: TEXT, INTRODUCTION, and NOTES. **1s. 6d.**

> PART II. A VOCABULARY (in order of the Text), with TEST PAPERS. *Interleaved*, **1s.**

> PART III.: A LITERAL TRANSLATION. **1s.**

> THE THREE PARTS COMPLETE. **2s. 6d.**

Horace, Odes, Book II. Edited by A. H. ALLCROFT, B.A. Oxon. and B. J. HAYES, M.A. Lond.

> PART I.: TEXT, INTRODUCTION, and NOTES. **1s. 6d.**

> PART II.: A VOCABULARY (in order of the Text), with TEST PAPERS. *Interleaved*, **1s.**

> PART III. A LITERAL TRANSLATION. **1s.**

> THE THREE PARTS COMPLETE. **2s. 6d.**

FOR JUNE, 1891.

(*Ready early in* 1890.)

Livy, Book I. Edited by A. H. ALLCROFT, B.A. Oxon., and W. F. MASOM, B.A. Lond.

> PART I.: TEXT, INTRODUCTION, and NOTES. **2s.**

> PART II.: A VOCABULARY (in order of the Text); with TEST PAPERS. *Interleaved*, **1s.**

> PART III.: A LITERAL TRANSLATION. **1s. 6d.**

> THE THREE PARTS COMPLETE. **3s. 6d.**

𝕿𝖍𝖊 𝕿𝖚𝖙𝖔𝖗𝖎𝖆𝖑 𝕾𝖊𝖗𝖎𝖊𝖘—𝕵𝖓𝖙𝖊𝖗. 𝕬𝖗𝖙𝖘.

INTERMEDIATE ARTS DIRECTORY, with FULL ANSWERS to the Examination Papers. No. II., 1889. 1s. 6d.

CONTENTS : Introductory Hints—University Regulations—Advice on the Choice of Text-Books (including Special Subjects for 1890)—**Examination Papers** set July, 1889—**Full Solutions** to *all* the above Examination Papers (except Special Subjects for the year) by the following Tutors of University Correspondence College :—

B. J. HAYES, M.A. Lond., First in First Class Honours in Classics at Inter. and Final B.A., Gold Medallist in Classics at M.A.

W.F.MASOM, B.A.Lond.,First Class Honours in Classics at B.A.,French and English Honours at Inter., 2nd in Honours at Matric., &c.

A. J. WYATT, M.A. Lond., Head of the M.A. List in English and French, Teacher's Diploma, etc.

L. J. LHUISSIER, B.A. Lond., First in Honours at Inter. and Final, B.-ès-Sc.,B.-ès-L.Paris, also of Stuttgart & Strasburg Universities.

H. E. JUST, B.A. Lond., Double Honours in French and German (1st Class), First in First Class Honours at Inter.

W. H. LOW, M.A. Lond. (German and English).

G. H. BRYAN, M.A., Fifth Wrangler, First Class, First Div. in Part II., Smith's Prizeman, Fellow of St. Peter's College, Cambridge.

" Students preparing for London University Degrees are recommended to see this little book, which is full of that particular kind of information so needful to those about to undergo examination. The article on ' Suitable Text Books for Private Students' is specially commendable."—*Teachers' Aid.*

" The 'Intermediate Arts Guide' contains an excellent selection of Text Books."—*Practical Teacher.*

"A really useful 'Intermediate Arts Guide,' than which nothing can be better for the private student who intends to present himself at the London University Examination of next July."—*School Guardian.*

The Intermediate Arts Directory for 1888, *with full Answers to all the Papers* (*including Special Subjects for the year*), *price* 2s. 6d., *may still be had.*

Intermediate Arts Examination Papers (in all subjects), 1889. 6d. (1888 can also be had.)

[*Published a week after each Examination.*

The Inter. Arts Exam. Papers for 1886 *and* 1887 (*with Answers to the Mathematical Questions*) *may still be had, price* 1s.

Intermediate Arts Book Guide, containing Advice to Private Students on the Choice of Text-Books in all subjects, including the Prescribed Authors. 6d.

The Tutorial Series—Inter. Arts.

Intermediate Latin. By W. F. MASOM, B.A. Lond., and B. J. HAYES, M.A. Lond. Second Edition, Enlarged. **2s. 6d.**

CONTENTS: Choice of Text-Books—Plan of Study for 30 weeks, with Notes and Hints on Grammar and Roman History—University Examination Papers in Grammar, Composition, and History from 1871 to 1889, with Model Answers to the Papers of 1888 and 1889—Illustrative Sentences for Latin Prose, &c.

London Undergraduate Unseens. A Reprint of all the Latin and Greek Passages set for Unprepared Translation at Matriculation and Intermediate Arts, together with schemes for reading in order of difficulty. **1s. 6d.**

History of the Reign of Augustus. By A. H. ALLCROFT, B.A. Oxon., and J. H. HAYDON, M.A. Camb. and Lond. **1s.**

Synopsis of Roman History to A.D. 96. **1s. 6d.** [*In preparation.*

Latin Honours Exam. Papers: A Reprint of the Papers in Grammar, History, and Geography set at the London Intermediate Examination in Arts (Honours), 1874—1888; together with all the B.A. (Honours) and M.A papers in Latin Grammar and Criticism. **3s. 6d.**

Intermediate Greek. By B. J. HAYES, M.A. Lond., and W. F. MASOM, B.A. Lond. **2s.**

CONTENTS: Advice on Text-Books—Plan of Study for 30 weeks, with indication of important points—Notes and Hints on Grammar, &c.—All the University Examination Papers in Grammar, with Model Answers to the last.

Notabilia of Anglo-Saxon Grammar. By A. J. WYATT, M.A. Lond. **1s. 6d.** (FOR HONOURS.)

Intermediate French Examination Papers, 1877 to 18. This collection contains *all* the Papers set in accordance with the present Regulations. **1s. 6d.**

Intermediate Mathematics. A GUIDE to the Mathematical Subjects prescribed for the Intermediate Examinations in ARTS and SCIENCE at the University of London. By the PRINCIPAL of University Correspondence College. *Second Edition.* **2s. 6d.**

CONTENTS: Advice on Text-Books—Scheme of Study for 30 weeks, with indication of important Book-work—30 Test Papers—100 Miscellaneous Questions—Directions for Revision—On the Structure of the University Examination Papers, and the relative importance of the several Mathematical Subjects—Answers to Test Papers—Examination Papers, with Model Answers, 1886 to 1888.

"There is no time lost in aimless efforts; the relative value of every part of the work is known at the outset; the mind is entirely relieved from the partial paralysis inseparable from uncertainty and doubtful gropings. Everything is 'cut and dry,' in the very best sense."—*Educational News.*

Coordinate Geometry. Part I. **2s.** [*In preparation.*

PUBLISHED BY W. B. CLIVE & CO., BOOKSELLERS ROW, STRAND.

The Tutorial Series—Inter. Arts, 1890.

Vergil—Georgics I. and II. A VOCABULARY (*interleaved*) in order of the Text, with TEST PAPERS. **1s.**

Vergil—Georgics I. and II. A TRANSLATION. By F. P. SHIP-HAM, M.A. Lond. **1s. 6d.**

Livy—Book XXI. Edited by A. H. ALLCROFT, B.A. and W. F. MASOM, B.A. Lond.

> PART I. INTRODUCTION, TEXT, and NOTES. **2s. 6d.**
>
> PART II. A VOCABULARY (*interleaved*) in order of the Text, with TEST PAPERS. **1s.**
>
> PART III. A TRANSLATION. **2s.**
>
> THE THREE PARTS COMPLETE. **4s. 6d.**

"Concise scholarly notes. . . . . The kind of help which is here offered is invaluable."—*Publishers' Circular*.

Sophocles—Antigone. Edited by A. H. ALLCROFT, B.A. and B. J. HAYES, M.A. Lond.

> PART I. INTRODUCTION, TEXT, and NOTES. **2s. 6d.**
>
> PART II. A VOCABULARY (*interleaved*) in order of the Text, with TEST PAPERS. **1s.**
>
> PART III. A TRANSLATION. **2s.**
>
> THE THREE PARTS COMPLETE. **4s. 6d.**

History of England, 1660 to 1714. By C. S. FEARENSIDE, B.A. Oxon., and W. H. LOW, M.A. Lond. **2s. 6d.**

Synopsis of English History, 1660 to 1714. **2s.**

History of English Literature, 1660 to 1714. By W. H. Low, M.A. Lond. **3s. 6d.**

Dryden.—Essay on Dramatic Poesy. 2s. With NOTES. **3s. 6d.**

Notes on Dryden's Essay on Dramatic Poesy. By W. H. Low, M.A. Lond. **2s.**

Notes on Addison's Essays on Milton. By W. H. Low, M.A. Lond. **2s.**

Intermediate English, 1890. QUESTIONS on all the Pass and Honours subjects set. **2s.**

Havelok the Dane. A close TRANSLATION into Modern English, preceded by the Additional Notes and Corrections issued in Prof. Skeat's new edition. By A. J. WYATT, M.A. Lond. (For HONOURS, 1890.) **3s.**

The Tutorial Series—Inter. Arts, 1891.

(Ready early in 1890.)

Vergil.—Aeneid, IX. and X. A VOCABULARY *(interleaved)* in order of the Text, with TEST PAPERS. **1s.**

Vergil.—Aeneid, IX. and X. A TRANSLATION. By A. A. IRWIN NESBITT, M.A. **1s. 6d.** [**Ready.**

Tacitus.—Annals, I. Edited by C. S. FEARENSIDE, B.A. Oxon., and W. F. MASOM, B.A. Lond.

> PART I. INTRODUCTION, TEXT, and NOTES. **2s. 6d.**
>
> PART II. A VOCABULARY *(interleaved)* in order of the Text, with TEST PAPERS. **1s.**
>
> PART III. A TRANSLATION. **2s.**
>
> THE THREE PARTS COMPLETE. **4s. 6d.**

Herodotus, VI. Edited by W. F. MASOM, B.A. Lond., and C. S. FEARENSIDE, B.A. Oxon.

> PART I. INTRODUCTION, TEXT, and NOTES. **3s. 6d.**
>
> PART II. A VOCABULARY *(interleaved)* in order of the Text, with TEST PAPERS. **1s.**
>
> PART III. A TRANSLATION. **2s.**
>
> THE THREE PARTS COMPLETE. **5s. 6d.**

History of England, 1485 to 1580. By C. S. FEARENSIDE, B.A. **2s. 6d.**

Synopsis of English History, 1485 to 1580. 1s.

History of English Literature, 1485 to 1580. 3s. 6d.

Shakespeare.—Henry VIII. INTRODUCTION and NOTES by W. H. Low, M.A. Lond. **2s.**

Intermediate English, 1891. Questions on all the Pass and Honours subjects set. **2s.**

Notes on Spenser's Shepherd's Calender, with an INTRODUCTION. By A. J. WYATT, M.A. Lond. (For HONOURS, 1891.) **2s.** [**Ready.**

The Tutorial Series.—B.A.

THE B.A. DIRECTORY, with FULL ANSWERS to the
Examination Papers. *Ready a fortnight after the Examination.* No. I., 1889. **2s.**

CONTENTS: Introductory Hints—University Regulations—Advice on the Choice of Text-Books (including Special Subjects for 1890)— **Examination Papers** set October, 1889—**Full Solutions** to *all* the above Examination Papers (except Special Subjects for the Year) by the following Tutors of University Correspondence College :—

B. J. HAYES, M.A. Lond., First in First Class Honours in Classics at Inter. and B.A., Gold Medallist in Classics at M.A.

W. F. MASOM, B.A. Lond., First Class Honours in Classics at B.A., French and English Honours at Inter., 2nd in Honours at Matric, &c.

A. H. ALLCROFT, B.A. Oxon., First Class Honours at Moderations and at Final Classical Exam.

A. J. WYATT, M.A. Lond., Head of the M.A. List in English and French, Teachers' Diploma, &c.

L. J. LHUISSIER, B.A. Lond., First in Honours at Inter. and Final, B.-ès-Sc., B.-ès-L. Paris, also of Stuttgart and Strasburg Universities.

G. H. BRYAN, M.A., Fifth Wrangler, First Class, First Div., in Part II., Smith's Prizeman, Fellow of St. Peter's College, Cambridge.

R. BRYANT, D.Sc. Lond., B.A. Lond., Assistant Examiner in Mathematics at London University.

J. WELTON, M.A. Lond., First of his year in Mental and Moral Science, bracketed First of the B.A.'s at Degree Exam.

" Full of useful hints."—*School Guardian.*

Model Solutions to B.A. Papers, 1888 (including Special
Subjects for the Year), by Graduates at the head of the degree lists in each department. *Second and cheaper issue.* **2s. 6d.**

"The kind of book a student should have by his side during his last weeks of preparation . . . . Concise, accurate, and complete."—*Board Teacher.*
"It is the first time we have seen so complete a set of answers in so excellent and readable a form."—*Practical Teacher.*

B.A. Examination Papers (in all Subjects), 1889. 6d.
Ready a fortnight after the Examination. B.A. Examination Papers for 1887 (with Answers to the Mathematical Questions and a Scheme for reading Mental and Moral Science), and for 1888 (with a Scheme for reading Classics), may still be had, price 1s. each set.

The B.A. Book Guide, containing Advice to Private Students on
the Choice of Text-Books in all Subjects, including the Prescribed Authors. **6d.**

14

The Tutorial Series. — B.A.

---◦◇◦---

B.A. Latin Examination Papers : being the QUESTIONS set at the London B.A. Examinations, 1871—1888 (excluding those on Prescribed Authors), with full Solutions to 1888, and Additional Questions. **2s.**

B.A. Greek Examination Papers : being the QUESTIONS set at the London B.A. Examinations, 1871—1887 (excluding those on Prescribed Authors), with Additional Questions. **2s.**

London B.A. Unseens : being all the PASSAGES set for TRANSLATION from Books not prescribed at the B.A. Examination of the University of London, together with Schemes for reading in order of difficulty. **2s.**

Synopsis of Roman History to A.D. 96. **1s. 6d.** [*In preparation.*

B.A. French. The PAPERS set at the London B.A. Examinations 1877—1888; with full SOLUTIONS to 1888, and Hints on Reading-Books, Grammar, &c., by A. J. WYATT, M.A. Lond. **2s.**

B.A. Mathematics : Questions and Solutions. Containing *all* the PASS PAPERS in Pure Mathematics given at the B.A. Examinations, including 1888, with complete SOLUTIONS; and an article on Suitable Books for Private Students. **3s. 6d.**

"The solutions are admirable, and cannot fail to be suggestive even to experienced mathematicians."—*Irish Teachers' Journal.*

"We can recommend this little volume to all whom it may concern."—*Practical Teacher.*

B.A. Mixed Mathematics : being the PAPERS set at the London B.A. Examinations, 1874—1888 ; with full SOLUTIONS to 1888, 200 Miscellaneous Examples, and Hints on Text-Books, by G. H. BRYAN, M.A. **2s.**

B.A. Mental and Moral Science. The PAPERS set at the London B.A. Examinations, 1874—1888; with SOLUTIONS to 1888, and an article on Text-Books suitable for Private Students, by J. WELTON, M.A. Lond. **2s.**

Notabilia of Anglo-Saxon Grammar, by A. J. WYATT, M.A. Lond. **1s. 6d.**

The Tutorial Series.—B.A., 1890.

B.A. Test Papers on Special Classics for 1890.—The AUTHORS and SPECIAL PERIODS in Latin and Greek. **2s.**

Cicero.—De Oratore. Book II. A TRANSLATION by a London GRADUATE in First Class Honours, Translator of *Sophocles' Electra* and *Demosthenes' Androtion.* **3s.**

Vergil.—Aeneid. Books VII.—X. A TRANSLATION. By A. A. IRWIN NESBITT, M.A. **2s.**

Synopsis of Roman History, A.D. 14—96, with short Biographies of eminent men, and a History of the Literature of the Period. By W. F. MASOM, B.A. Lond., and A. H. ALLCROFT, B.A. **1s.**

Aristophanes.—Plutus. Expurgated TEXT, INTRODUCTION, and NOTES. By M. T. QUINN, M.A. Lond. **3s. 6d.**

Aristophanes.—Plutus. A TRANSLATION by M. T. QUINN, M.A. Lond. **2s.**

Aristophanes.—Plutus. TEXT, NOTES, and TRANSLATION (complete). By M. T. QUINN, M.A. Lond. **5s.**

Thucydides.—Book IV. A TRANSLATION. By G. F. H. SYKES, B.A. Lond., Assistant-Examiner in Classics at Lond. Univ. **2s. 6d.**

A Synopsis of Grecian History, B.C. 405—358, with short Biographies of the chief Writers and Statesmen of the Period. By W. F. MASOM, B.A. Lond., and A. H. ALLCROFT, B.A. **1s.**

Dan Michel.— Ayenbite of Inwit. A TRANSLATION of the more difficult passages (including the whole of pp. 1—48), by A. J. WYATT, M.A. Lond. **3s.**

The Saxon Chronicle, from 800 to 1001 A.D. A TRANSLATION by W. H. LOW, M.A. Lond. **3s.**

B.A. English Examination Questions on all the Pass Subjects set for 1890. **2s.**

The Tutorial Series.—B.A., 1891.

(Ready early in 1890.)

B.A. Latin Notabilia and Test Papers for 1891, on the Prescribed AUTHORS and SPECIAL PERIOD of History. **1s. 6d.**

B.A. Greek Notabilia and Test Papers for 1891, on the Prescribed AUTHORS and SPECIAL PERIOD, including a List of the more difficult Greek Verbal Forms. **1s. 6d.**

Cicero.—De Finibus, Book I. Edited with Explanatory NOTES and an INTRODUCTION. **3s. 6d.**

Cicero.—De Finibus, Book I. A TRANSLATION. **2s.**

Cicero.—De Finibus, Book I. TEXT, NOTES, and TRANSLATION (*complete*). **5s.**

Terence.—Adelphi. A TRANSLATION. **2s.**

History of the Reigns of Augustus and Tiberius, with an account of the Literature of the Period. By A. H. ALLCROFT, M.A. Oxon., and W. F. MASOM, B.A. Lond. **2s. 6d.**

Synopsis of Roman History, B.C. 31—A.D. 37, with short Biographies of Eminent Men. By W. F. MASOM, B.A. Lond., and A. H. ALLCROFT, B.A. Oxon. **1s.**

Euripides. — Iphigenia in Tauris. A TRANSLATION. By G. F. H. SYKES, B.A. Lond., Assistant-Examiner in Classics at the University of London. **2s. 6d.** [*Immediately.*

Plato.—Phaedo. A TRANSLATION. **3s. 6d.**

History of Sicily, B.C. 490—289, from the Tyranny of Gelon to the Death of Agathocles, with a History of Literature. By A. H. ALLCROFT, B.A., and W. F. MASOM, B.A. Lond. **3s. 6d.** [*Immediately.*

Synopsis of Sicilian History, B.C. 491—289. By A. H. ALLCROFT, B.A., and W. F. MASOM, B.A. Lond. **1s.**

B.A. English Examination Questions on all the Pass Subjects set for 1891. **2s.**

Tutorial Series—Inter. Sc. and Prel. Sci.

Inter. Science and Prelim. Sci. Guide. No. I., July, 1889. **1s.**

CONTENTS: Introductory Hints—Advice on the Choice of Text-books by the Authors of Science Model Answers (*see below*)—The University Regulations—The Papers set at the Examination.

Science Model Answers: being Solutions to the INTERMEDIATE SCIENCE and PRELIMINARY SCIENTIFIC Examination Papers set July, 1889. **3s. 6d.** *The Papers are answered by*—

S. RIDEAL, D.Sc. Lond., Gold Medallist in Chemistry at B.Sc., Assistant Examiner to the Science and Art Department.

H. M. FERNANDO, M.B., B.Sc. Lond., Second in First Class Honours Zoology, and Third in Honours Botany at Inter. Sc. and Prel. Sci., First Class Honours (deserving of Scholarship) in Physiology at B.Sc.; Gold Medal in Physiology and First Class Honours in Chemistry at Int. M.B.; Two Gold Medals at M.B.

R. W. STEWART, B.Sc. Lond., First in First Class Honours in Chemistry at Inter. Sc., and First in First Class Honours in Physics at B.Sc.

W. H. THOMAS, B.Sc. Lond., First in First Class Honours in Chemistry.

G. H. BRYAN, M.A., Fifth Wrangler and Smith's Prizeman, Fellow of St. Peter's College, Cambridge.

J. H. DIBB, B.Sc. Lond., Double Honours, Mathematics and Physics.

Science Physics Papers: being the Questions set at the London Intermediate Science and Preliminary Scientific Examinations for Twenty-one years, with full Answers to the 1889 Papers, by R. W. STEWART, B.Sc. Lond. **3s. 6d.**

Science Biology Papers: being the Questions set at the London Intermediate Science and Preliminary Scientific Examinations for Twelve Years (those not bearing on the present Syllabus being denoted by an asterisk), with supplementary Questions and full Answers to the 1889 Paper, and Advice as to Text-books, by H. M. FERNANDO, M.B., B.Sc. Lond. **3s. 6d.**

Science Chemistry Papers: being the Questions set at the London Intermediate Science and Preliminary Scientific Examinations for Twenty-one years, with full Answers to the 1889 Papers, and Advice as to Text-books, by W. H. THOMAS, B.Sc. Lond., and R. W. STEWART, B.Sc. Lond. **3s. 6d.**

Analysis of a Simple Salt, with a selection of model Analyses. **2s.** [*In preparation.*

Intermediate Mathematics. (For Inter. Sc.) *Second edition.* **2s. 6d.**

LATIN.

Caesar.—Gallic War, Book VII. VOCABULARIES in order of the Text, with TEST PAPERS. **6d.**; interleaved, **9d.**

Cicero, Pro Cluentio. A TRANSLATION. By J. LOCKEY, M.A. Lond. **2s.**

Cicero, Pro Cluentio. VOCABULARIES in order of the Text, with TEST PAPERS. Interleaved, **1s.**

Horace, The Epistles. A TRANSLATION. By W. F. MASOM, B.A. Lond. **2s.**

Horace, The Epistles. VOCABULARIES in order of the Text, with TEST PAPERS. Interleaved, **1s.**

Juvenal.—Satires III., X., XI. A TRANSLATION by a Gold Medallist in Classics at London M.A. **2s.**

Sallust.—Catiline. VOCABULARIES in order of the Text, with TEST PAPERS. **6d.**; interleaved, **9d.**

Vergil.—Aeneid, Book I. VOCABULARIES in order of the Text, with TEST PAPERS. **6d.**; interleaved, **9d.**

Vergil.—Aeneid, Book I. A Literal TRANSLATION. **1s.**

Vergil.—Aeneid, Book IV. A Close TRANSLATION. **1s.**

Vergil.—Aeneid, Book V. VOCABULARIES in order of the Text, with TEST PAPERS. **6d.**; interleaved, **9d.**

Vergil.—Aeneid, Book V. A Literal TRANSLATION. **1s.**

A Synopsis of Roman History, 63 B.C.—14 A.D., with short Biographies of the Chief Writers of the Period. By W. F. MASOM, B.A. Lond. **1s.**

GREEK.

Aeschylus.—Agamemnon. A TRANSLATION by a Gold Medallist in Classics at London M.A. **2s.**

Demosthenes.—Androtion. A TRANSLATION. By a London GRADUATE in First Class Honours. **2s.**

GREEK—*continued.*

Homer.—Iliad, Book VI. Edited by B. J. Hayes, M.A. Lond.

> PART I.: Text, Introduction, and Notes, with an Appendix on the Homeric Dialect. **1s. 6d.**
>
> PART II.: Vocabularies in order of the Text, with Test Papers. Interleaved, **1s.**
>
> PART III.: A Translation. **1s.**
>
> *The Three Parts complete.* **2s. 6d.**

Homer, Odyssey XVII. Text, Introduction, and Notes. By W. F. Masom, B.A. Lond. **2s.**

Homer, Odyssey XVII. A Translation, with an Appendix on the Homeric Dialect. **2s.**

Homer, Odyssey XVII. Vocabularies in order of the Text, with Test Papers. Interleaved, **1s.**

Homer, Odyssey XVII. Complete. Introduction, Text, and Notes — Vocabularies — Test Papers — Translation — Appendix. **5s.**

Sophocles.—Electra. A Translation. By a London Graduate in First Class Honours. **2s.**

Xenophon.—Cyropaedeia, Book I. Vocabularies in order of the Text, with Test Papers. **9d.** Interleaved, **1s.**

Xenophon.—Cyropaedeia, Book V. Vocabularies in order of the Text, with Test Papers. Interleaved, **1s.**

Xenophon.—Oeconomicus. A Translation by B. J. Hayes, M.A. Lond. **3s.**

"This translation deserves the praise of painstaking accuracy."—*Practical Teacher.*

"Private students will welcome the assistance afforded by this valuable addition to the 'Tutorial Series."—*Teachers' Aid.*

GREEK—continued.

A Synopsis of Grecian History, B.C. 382—338, with short Biographies of the Chief Writers and Statesmen of the Period. By W. F. MASOM, B.A. Lond. **1s.**

Test-Papers on Classics. CICERO PRO SESTIO; JUVENAL; AESCHYLUS' AGAMEMNON; XENOPHON'S OECONOMICUS; ROMAN HISTORY, B.C. 63–A.D. 14; GRECIAN HISTORY, B.C. 382–338. **2s.**

ENGLISH.

Alfred's Orosius. A Literal TRANSLATION of the more difficult passages. **2s. 6d.**

Glossaries to Alfred's Orosius. 1s.

Milton's Sonnets. With an Introduction to each Sonnet, and Notes, together with an account of the History and Construction of the *Sonnet*, and Examination Questions. By W. F. MASOM, B.A. Lond. **1s. 6d.**

"This useful little book."—*Practical Teacher.*

"This book will be a great help to those who are preparing for the forthcoming Intermediate Examination in Arts at the University of London."—*Educational Times.*

Questions on English History and Literature. FIRST SERIES (300); History of England, 1625 to 1666 (97); English Literature, 1625 to 1666 (57); "King John" (31); Milton (47); "Religio Medici" (24); Morris and Skeat's Extracts (44). **2s.**

Questions on English Literature. SECOND SERIES (363); English Literature, 1558 to 1603 (74); Havelok the Dane (49); "Julius Caesar" (49); "Shepherd's Calender" (32); Sweet's Anglo-Saxon Primer (159). **2s.**

TUTORS OF
UNIVERSITY CORRESPONDENCE COLLEGE.

The following Tutors are on the regular staff of University Correspondence College, and engage in no other teaching:—

A. J. WYATT, Esq., M.A. Lond., First of his year in Branch IV. (English and French), Teachers' Diploma, Early English Text Society's Prizeman ; Author of *Notes on the Shepherd's Calender*, *Notabilia of Anglo-Saxon Grammar*, a Translation of *Havelok the Dane*, *Agenbite of Inwit*, &c.

B. J. HAYES, Esq., M.A. Lond., First in First Class Honours in Classics both at Inter. and B.A., Gold Medallist in Classics at M.A. ; Editor of *Homer's Iliad VI.* ; Author of *Matric. Latin*, *Intermediate Greek*, a Translation of *Xenophon's Oeconomicus*, &c.

G. H. BRYAN, Esq., M.A., Fifth Wrangler, First Class, First Division in Part II., Smith's Prizeman, Fellow of St. Peter's College, Cambridge ; Author of *B.A. Mathematics, Coordinate Geometry*.

Mons. L. J. LHUISSIER, B.A. Lond., First in Honours both at Inter. and Final; B.-ès-Sc. and B.-ès-L. Paris; also of Stuttgart and Strasburg Universities.

J. WELTON, Esq., M.A. Lond., First of his year in Mental and Moral Science, bracketed equal as First of the B.A.'s at Degree Exam., Honours in French at B.A. and 4th of twenty-seven in English Honours at Inter.

R. W. STEWART, Esq., B.Sc. Lond., First in First Class Honours in Chemistry at Inter. Science, and First in First Class Honours in Physics at B.Sc. ; Author of *A Text-Book of Heat and Light.*

C. W. C. BARLOW, Esq., M.A., Sixth Wrangler, First Class, First Div., in Part II. Math. Tripos, late Scholar of St. Peter's College, Cambridge, Mathematical Honourman at Inter. Arts, Lond.

W. F. MASOM, Esq., B.A. Lond., First Class Honours (Classics) at B.A., French and English Honours at Inter. Arts, Second in Honours at Matric., University Exhibitioner; Editor of *Herodotus VI.* ; Author of a Translation of *The Epistles of Horace ;* *Inter. Latin ; Synopses of Roman and Grecian History.*

H. J. MAIDMENT, Esq., B.A. Oxon. and Lond., First Class Honours.

A. H. JOHNSON, Esq., B.A. Lond., First Class Honours, University Prizeman in English.

W. H. THOMAS, Esq., B.Sc. Lond., First in First Class Honours in Chemistry.

J. H. DIBB, Esq., B.Sc. Lond., Double Honours, Mathematics and Physics.

W. H. LOW, Esq., M.A. Lond. (German and English) ; Author of *A History of English Literature*, *A Translation of the Saxon Chronicle*, *Notes on Dryden's Essay on Dramatic Poesy*, *Notes on Addison's Essays on Milton*, &c.

C. S. FEARENSIDE, Esq., B.A. Oxon., Honourman in Mod. History and Classics (1st Class) ; Author of *A History of England*, 1660 *to* 1714.

R. O. B. KERIN, Esq., B.A. Lond., First in First Class Honours in Classics.

TUTORS OF UNIV. CORR. COLL.—*continued.*

H. M. GRINDON, Esq., M.A. Lond., Classical Honourman.

C. P. F. O'DWYER, Esq., B.A. Lond., Classical Honourman.

T. THRELFALL, Esq., M.A. Oxon., Double Honours Natural Science and Mathematics (First Class).

H. K. TOMPKINS, Esq., B.Sc. Lond., F C.S., F.I.C., Honourman in Chemistry.

F. P. SHIPHAM, Esq., M.A. Lond., Classical Honourman.

E. M. JONES, Esq., B.A., Mathematical Honours.

A. A. IRWIN NESBITT, Esq., M.A., Classical Honours, late Professor M. A. O. College, Aligarh, India, Author of A Translation of *Virgil's Aeneid.*

S. MOSES, Esq., M.A. Oxon., B.A. Lond., First Class Hons. Lond. and Oxon. (Double), Latin Exhibitioner at Int. Arts, First in Honours at Matriculation ; Assistant Examiner at London University ; Editor of *Cicero De Amicitiâ, Pro Balbo*, and *De Finibus I.*

A. H. ALLCROFT, Esq., B.A. Oxon., First Class Classical Honours at Moderations and Final Classical Exam. ; Editor of *Livy XXI., Sophocles' Antigone, Horace' Odes ;* Author of *A History of Sicily, The Reign of Augustus, Latin Syntax and Composition.*

Additional Tutors for Special Subjects.

F. RYLAND, Esq., M.A., Second in First Class Honours (Mental and Moral Science, &c.) ; Examiner for the Moral Sciences Tripos, Cambridge ; Author of a *Manual of Psychology and Ethics for Lond. B.A. and B.Sc.*, &c.

ROBERT BRYANT, Esq., D.Sc. Lond., B.A. Lond., Assistant Examiner in Mathematics at London University.

J. H. HAYDON, Esq., M.A. Camb. and Lond., Exhibitioner in Latin at Inter. Arts, Univ. Scholar in Classics at B.A., Gold Medallist at M.A. ; First Class, First Div., Classical Tripos.

G. F. H. SYKES, Esq., B.A. Lond., Classical Honours, Assistant Examiner in Classics at Lond. Univ ; Author of a Translation of *Thucydides IV.*, and *Iphigenia in Tauris.*

HEINRICH BAUMANN, Esq., M.A. Lond., First in First Class Honours at Inter. and Final B.A. both in French and German.

W. H. EVANS, Esq., B.Sc., M.D. Lond., First Class Honours at M.B.

SAMUEL RIDEAL, Esq., D.Sc. (Chemistry), Gold Medallist ; Assistant Examiner to the Science and Art Department.

J. W. EVANS, Esq., B.Sc., LL.B. Lond.; First in First Class Hons.

C. H. DRAPER, Esq., D.Sc., B.A., Teachers' Diploma.

A. H. WALKER, Esq., D.Mus. Lond., 10th in Honours at Matriculation, and Honours in Classical Tripos.

G. W. HILL, Esq., B.Sc. (Hons.), M.B. (Hons.).

H. E. JUST, Esq., B.A. Lond., Double Honours in French and German (1st Class), First in First Class Honours at Inter.

CHIEF SUCCESSES

University Correspondence College.

AT MATRICULATION, JUNE, 1889,

78 U. C. Coll. Students passed.

This number far exceeds the largest ever passed by any other Institution at this Examination.

AT INTER. ARTS, 1889,

71 U. C. Coll. Students passed,

(A number altogether unprecedented);

Eleven in Honours, two with first places, and one with a second place.

21 also passed the Inter. Sc. and Prel. Sci. Exams.,

five in Honours.

AT B.A., 1889,

70 U. C. Coll. Students passed;

Being a larger number than was ever before passed by any Institution.

16 U. C. Coll. Students took Honours.

6 also passed at B.Sc., 2 of whom headed Honour lists.

AT M.A., 1889,

Two Students of Univ. Corr. Coll.

passed in Branch I., and in 1888

One headed the Mental and Moral Science List.

Full Prospectus, Pass Lists, and further information may be had on application to the

SECRETARY, 12½ Booksellers Row, Strand, W.C.

ImTheStory.com

CPSIA information can be obtained at www.ICGtesting.com
Printed in the USA
LVOW01s2010280714

396388LV00027B/1158/P